Slow Cooker

Lose Weight Forever

ULTIMATE SLOW COOKER DIET FOR BEGINNERS,
THE HEALTHY, FAST AND NATURAL WAY TO LOSE WEIGHT

Martina Slajerova

FAIR WINDS

Quarto.com

First Published in 2018 by Fair Winds, an imprint of
The Quarto Group,
100 Cummings Center, Suite 265-D, Beverly, MA 01915, USA.
T (978) 282-9590 F (978) 283-2742

28 27 26 25 24 1 2 3 4 5

ISBN: 978-0-7603-9332-1

The content in this book was originally published as *Keto Slow Cooker & One-Pot Meals* by Martina Slajerova (Fair Winds Press 2018).

Library of Congress Cataloging-in-Publication Data available under *Keto Slow Cooker & One-Pot Meals* by Martina Slajerova.

Design and Page Layout: Rita Sowins / Sowins Design
Photography: Martina Slajerova
Top right cover image by Shutterstock.

Printed in China

Contents

INTRODUCTION

Before I discovered low-carb eating, I followed what most people considered to be a healthy lifestyle. The general advice was to eat less, avoid dietary fats, and exercise more. So it was only natural that I was following a mostly vegetarian low-fat diet. I was eating plenty of vegetables, fruits, and whole grains, yet I had zero energy and I was always hungry. I was a sugar burner. I kept struggling with my weight even though I was exercising almost every day. I couldn't understand why I was feeling so bad because I thought I had done everything I possibly could to stay healthy. Looking back, I can't believe how wrong I was!

What Is the Ketogenic Diet?

The ketogenic diet is a high-fat, moderate-protein, low-carb diet. It's a diet that causes ketones to be produced by the liver, shifting the body's metabolism away from glucose and toward fat utilization. Essentially, your body switches from glucose to fat as the primary fuel. When that happens, it produces molecules known as ketones. (That's where the word *keto* comes from.) The ketogenic diet is not a new concept. It has, in fact, been used for treating epilepsy and other neurological diseases since the 1920s. A well-formulated ketogenic diet can not only help you lose weight, but it can also improve and help treat or manage several health conditions, such as high blood pressure, hormone issues, diabetes, Alzheimer's, Parkinson's, epilepsy, and even cancer.

For me it's not a diet, it's a lifestyle. Studies in *Obesity Reviews* (Santos, et al., 2012) and *New England Journal of Medicine* (Foster, et al., 2003; Samaha, et al., 2003) have shown that low-carb diets outperform other diets in terms of weight loss and health benefits. Unlike other dietary approaches, once you learn the basic principles, it's easy to follow and it's easy to stick with in the long term. You will enjoy the food because fat tastes good and will keep you fuller for longer. I've been following the ketogenic diet for more than five years and I never looked back because I don't ever feel like I am dieting.

A well-formulated ketogenic diet focuses on the amount of carbohydrates *and* on food quality. There is no place for processed foods, artificial sweeteners, and foods laden with unhealthy additives. I rarely buy any packaged foods, especially those with never-ending lists of ingredients and names most people can't even pronounce. A well-formulated ketogenic diet includes healthy low-carb foods, such as non-starchy vegetables, avocados, fatty fish, meat, eggs, and full-fat dairy (if you can tolerate dairy).

Why the Slow Cooker?

Life gets busier and busier. People spend more time at work and less time with their families. Cooking and eating together has become a rare occasion. Eating healthy without spending hours in the kitchen has been challenging for most of us. Don't get me wrong, I love cooking and I enjoy it every time. But I don't expect everyone else to be as enthusiastic as I am, and we all have different priorities. Just like many of you, there are days when I don't have more than fifteen minutes to prepare a meal, and that's when I fire up my slow cooker! I've been using it to prepare healthy keto meals for several years, and it has become a lifesaver.

My aim is to show you that no matter how busy your life gets, you should always find time to eat healthy, even if it means that you don't have more than a few minutes to prepare a meal. Like my *Quick Keto Meals in 30 Minutes or Less* cookbook, this book is full of quick and easy meals that can be cooked by anyone—even a complete novice.

{ Chapter 1 }

SLOW COOKING 101

How Does a Slow Cooker Work?

A slow cooker, also known as a Crock-Pot, consists of three main parts: an electric heating element, a cooking dish (stoneware in most cases), and a lid. In a slow cooker, heat is distributed from the bottom and transferred all the way up the stoneware dish. As the food heats up, the steam generated by the heat creates a vacuum seal with the lid.

The slow cooker is an ideal gadget for every busy cook. Food gets cooked very slowly, typically for 4 to 8 hours depending on the temperature setting. Liquids do not evaporate and that's why you can safely keep your slow cooker on all day without supervision. Once your meal is done, most slow cookers switch to a "keep warm" mode so that you can enjoy a warm dinner when you get back from work.

Benefits of Slow Cooking

TIME SAVER

A slow cooker can provide warming comfort meals and, for those of us who are always busy, it offers the convenience of cooking without all the time-consuming hassle. It can be such a lifesaver when we are short of time and just want to make a big batch of *something* to keep us going throughout the week. You can literally spend just five minutes prepping the ingredients in the morning, throw them in the slow cooker, set the timer, and wait for the magic to happen. When you get home from work, dinner is ready to be served!

MONEY SAVER

Cooking in a slow cooker is budget-friendly for several reasons. First, electric slow cookers are widely available and affordable. The slow cooker also enables you to cook tough, inexpensive meat cuts, such as brisket, chuck, shin, shanks, and oxtails, turning them into hearty stews and wholesome curries. Finally, slow cookers are energy-efficient and waste less energy compared to a traditional oven. It's also likely you will cook meat and sides together instead of having to prepare them separately on the stove or in the oven. It's a win-win!

HEALTHY COOKING

Poaching and braising is by far the healthiest way to prepare foods, especially if you're using the lowest setting on your slow cooker. Low cooking temperatures help retain more vitamins and minerals. Plus, tough meat cuts contain the largest amount of connective tissue high in collagen and elastin. Collagen is transformed into gelatin by cooking. It has several benefits:

- It can keep your joints, ligaments, tendons, and bones healthy, and it can reduce joint pain.
- It's good for your gut and helps with intestinal permeability, a.k.a. "leaky gut."
- It's great for thyroid health and helps fight adrenal fatigue. Collagen is especially great for women with thyroid issues.

Step-by-Step Guide to Slow Cooking

PREPARE THE INGREDIENTS

Preheat the slow cooker while you prepare the ingredients. Most slow cooker recipes require basic prep work, such as slicing the vegetables and adding everything to the slow cooker. Browning and searing the meat and vegetables before slow cooking them is optional, but it will enhance the flavor of your dish.

WHEN COOKING IN A SLOW COOKER, THE ORDER MATTERS

1. Start by layering the firm vegetables, such as rutabaga and turnip, on the bottom.
2. Top with meat. You can use a large variety of meats, such as beef brisket, short ribs, chuck, pork shoulder, and lamb leg or shanks. Apart from tough meat cuts, you can use ground meat, chicken, fish, and seafood.
3. Add aromatics, such as onion, garlic, lemon juice, chiles, ginger, celery, and peppers, and add liquid ingredients, such as tomato puree, bone broth, or stock.
4. Add herbs and spices, such as paprika, cumin, chili powder, cinnamon, coriander, basil, oregano, thyme, rosemary, or parsley. Herbs will lose their flavor after prolonged cooking, and it's good to add some more near the end of the cooking process.

5. Some vegetables may overcook and become mushy. If using medium-tender vegetables, such as broccoli and cauliflower, add them in the last 2 to 4 hours of the cooking process. If using soft vegetables, such as zucchini or chard, add them to the slow cooker near the end of the cooking process, during the last 1 to 2 hours.
6. Add dairy, such as cream, cheese, sour cream, and cream cheese, and coconut milk and cream, at the end of the cooking process, in the last 15 to 30 minutes. Prolonged cooking may result in the sauce breaking.

AVOID COMMON MISTAKES

Do

- Preheat the slow cooker. If you start with a cold slow cooker, you will need to add an extra 15 to 20 minutes to your cooking time.
- Use the right temperature setting. Typically, there are two temperature settings. The rule of thumb is to cook tender meats, such as chicken and fish, on a low temperature setting for 2 to 6 hours (depending on type and size). Cook tough meat cuts, such as brisket and shoulder, on low for 6 to 8 hours or on high for 3 to 4 hours (in some cases even longer). *Warning:* Not all slow cookers are equal. After trying three different brands, I realized that the temperature settings were not the same across all three of them. It may take some trial and error to get the temperature setting right, especially when making delicate recipes like cakes.
- If you are cooking a large meat cut that is more than 3 pounds (1.4 kg), cut it in half to ensure even cooking.
- If you are busy in the morning, prepare everything the night before, place it in the slow cooker dish, cover, and store in the fridge. When you wake up, take it out from the fridge and leave it on the kitchen counter for 15 to 20 minutes. This will allow the ingredients to come closer to room temperature before cooking in the slow cooker.
- Use a thermometer to check when your meat is cooked, especially if you cook large cuts of meat.
- If cooking tough meat cuts that require 6 to 8 hours of cooking, add most vegetables in the last 2 to 4 hours of the cooking process. Also, avoid cutting vegetables too small or they will overcook.
- Keep your food safe. Don't leave the food in the slow cooker once it's cooked. Let it cool down, place in airtight containers, and refrigerate or freeze. Most slow cookers will automatically switch to a "keep warm" mode that will keep the dish warm for a few more hours without spoiling, but it may overcook the dish if used for too long.
- Are you short on time? Simplify the preparation process! You can skip browning the vegetables and meat. Although browning is great for boosting the flavor, it is not essential in most recipes. Just throw all the ingredients in a slow cooker and let it do its job.

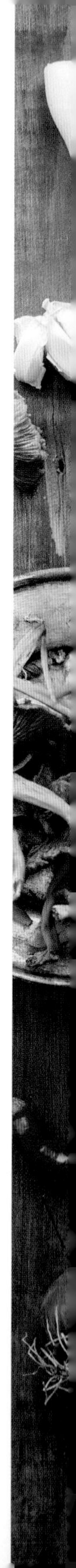

- Do you have leftover juices from last night's roasts? Use them to cook your vegetables to boost flavor and nothing goes to waste.
- Use leftover bones and cartilage to make homemade stock (page 22) or broth (page 33). Place them in a freezer bag and make a batch when you collect enough bones.
- Buy cheap meat cuts. The beauty of having a slow cooker is that you can transform inexpensive meat cuts, such as chuck and brisket, into delectable meals.
- Foods cooked at high altitudes take longer to cook. If you live at high altitude, add an additional 1 hour for every 2 hours of cooking.
- If converting your favorite recipe for the slow cooker, be sure to pick the right recipe. Most soups, stews, and casseroles are guaranteed to work. Pay extra attention if converting a dessert.

Don't

- Do not underfill or overfill your slow cooker. Ideally, your slow cooker should be at least half full and no more than three-quarters full.
- Do not use frozen meat and vegetables. They slow down the cooking process and create an ideal environment for bacteria to thrive.
- Go easy on the liquids. Slow cookers have very little to no evaporation. If you're adapting a stove-top recipe, you will need to reduce the amount of liquids. You can always add more water or liquids near the end of the cooking process if the sauce is too thick. Some recipes, such as Beef Short Ribs (page 63), will only need ¼ cup (60 ml) of water. Using too much water will, in fact, draw more moisture from meat and will dry it out. Desserts and sweet treats need extra attention. It's easy to get the liquids wrong, and your cake will be too moist or too dry.
- When the cooking is in progress, do not open the lid unless you need to add more ingredients (e.g., large roasts will need longer to cook compared to tender vegetables). If you do have to remove the lid (and in some cases you will need to), add 20 to 30 minutes to the cooking time.
- Do not use whole nuts when making a dessert that includes liquids. Whole nuts will soak up all the liquids and will become unpalatable. Recipes with little to no liquids are fine.
- Don't touch the outside casing of the slow cooker when it's in process. It becomes very hot and you should only touch it with oven mitts. For the same reason, be sure to keep your cooker away from curtains, walls, and any other flammable items.
- Don't place the hot ceramic bowl directly on your kitchen counter. Always place it on a cooling rack.

Healthy Keto Cooking

COOK WITH HEALTHY FATS

You should pay extra attention to fats because most of your calories should come from them. Unhealthy fats can do as much damage as excessive carbohydrates.

Healthy Cooking Fats

Use oils and fats high in saturated fats (SFA), such as pastured lard, grass-fed beef tallow, chicken fat, duck fat, goose fat, clarified butter or ghee, butter, virgin coconut oil, and sustainably sourced palm kernel oil.

Fats Suitable for Light Cooking and Cold Use

Oils high in monounsaturated fats (MUFA), such as extra-virgin olive oil, avocado oil, and macadamia nut oil, are best for cold use, stir-fries, finishing meals, or after cooking.

Fats Only Suitable for Cold Use

Oils high in polyunsaturated fats (PUFA) are only suitable for cold use, such as in salad dressings and mayonnaise (page 19). These include nut and seed oils such as walnut, almond, hazelnut, flaxseed, sesame seed, or pumpkin seed oil. When you use oils high in omega-6 fatty acids, increase your intake of omega-3 fatty acids, especially from animal sources.

Always Avoid

Not all fats are suitable for a healthy, low-carb diet and, unfortunately, the most commonly used oils are unhealthy. All of the following options should be avoided: vegetable oils and shortening; hydrogenated and partially hydrogenated oils; margarine; and sunflower, canola, safflower, soy, cottonseed, or grapeseed oil. They are highly processed, inflammatory, and prone to oxidation.

What Does Eating "ad libitum" Mean?

When following a ketogenic diet, you should be eating to satiety (ad libitum). Aim for an adequate protein intake and use fat as a "filler" to sate your appetite while keeping carbs low, at 20 to 30 grams of net carbs. It's true that most people following the ketogenic diet don't need to count calories because they don't feel hungry and overeating is unlikely. The ketogenic diet is about getting the right amount of protein and fat to suit your individual needs: some people may be doing well on a diet with 60 percent of calories from fat while others may do better with a higher fat intake (typically during weight maintenance). Keep in mind that what matters is not relative percentages but grams of fat and protein per day. If you want to find out your ideal calorie intake, visit my blog at ketodietapp.com/blog/page/KetoDiet-Buddy.

CHOOSE YOUR PROTEINS WISELY

Just like fats, proteins play an important role in a healthy keto diet. Always buy the best quality of protein sources you can afford.

Meat & Eggs

When it comes to meat, quality matters. If your budget allows it, opt for organic eggs and grass-fed, humanely raised meat. Grass-fed beef contains more micronutrients and more omega-3 fatty acids. Additionally, pasture-raised and grass-fed animals have a much better quality of life compared to those kept in large industrial facilities. There is no need to splurge on expensive meat cuts to get quality tender meat. Opt for the "less desirable" beef brisket, chuck roast, pork shoulder, or lamb shanks.

Warning: When using raw eggs (Quick Mayonnaise, page 19), you should use only fresh, clean, properly refrigerated grade A or AA eggs with intact shells due to the slight risk of salmonella and other foodborne illnesses. Avoid contact between the yolks or whites and the outside of the shell. Prevent any risks by using eggs with pasteurized shells.

To pasteurize eggs at home, simply pour enough water in a saucepan to cover the eggs. Heat to about 140°F (60°C). Using a spoon, slowly place the eggs in the saucepan. Keep the eggs in the water for about 3 minutes. This should be enough to pasteurize the eggs and kill any potential bacteria. Let the eggs cool down and store in the fridge for 6 to 8 weeks.

Fish & Seafood

Avoid farmed fish and opt for wild-caught, locally sourced, sustainable fish. Imported farmed fish are exposed to antibiotics and chemicals, and they are often stored in bacteria-laden ice. Many species of fish have become overfished due to destructive harvesting methods that have a direct effect on the marine life.

And it doesn't end there. Our oceans are polluted and mercury levels in fish are higher than ever. Mercury is known to accumulate in fish and is dangerous to humans, especially pregnant women and young children, because it can damage the central nervous system. As a general rule, large fish that are higher up in the food chain are more likely to contain higher levels of mercury. The smaller the fish, the lower the mercury levels.

So what's your best choice? Some of the best options according to the Seafood Watch Best Choices list are: Pacific sardines, Atlantic mackerel, freshwater Coho salmon, Alaskan salmon, canned salmon, Albacore tuna, and sablefish/black cod. All of the above are low in mercury and good sources of omega-3 fatty acids. To learn more about sustainable fish low in mercury, visit seafoodwatch.org and get the free Seafood Watch app.

What is Adequate Protein Intake?

According to Jeff Volek, Ph.D., R.D., and Stephen Phinney, M.D., Ph.D., best-selling authors of *The Art and Science of Low Carbohydrate Performance*, you will need between 0.6 and 1 gram per pound (1.3 to 2.2 grams per kilogram) of lean mass. In most cases, this translates to 65 to 80 grams of protein per day, sometimes even more. The exact amount depends on gender, lean mass weight, and activity level.

Don't get obsessed over your protein intake. Eating slightly more protein will not kick you out of ketosis or impair your progress. Studies in the *American Physiological Society* (Jahoor, et al., 1990) and *The Journal of Clinical Endocrinology & Metabolism* (Bisschop, et al., 2000) have shown that you would have to be eating huge amounts of protein to go into gluconeogenesis (converting protein to glucose). Remember, protein is the most sating macronutrient; it will help you feel less hungry and eat fewer calories. When you eat a high-protein meal, you body releases glucagon, which counterbalances insulin and plays a significant role in satiety. That's why it's imperative to eat adequate amount of protein if your aim is to lose body fat.

This doesn't mean that you should overeat protein. Protein is not a particularly efficient fuel source and too much of it may raise your insulin levels. If you are insulin resistant or diabetic, be aware that not all protein sources are equal and some, such as whey protein, will cause greater insulin responses than others. Also, those who suffer from diabetic nephropathy, a type of kidney disease caused by diabetes, will need to eat less protein.

CARBOHYDRATES ON THE KETOGENIC DIET

When following a ketogenic diet, you should aim for no more than 50 grams of total carbohydrates (20 to 30 grams of net carbohydrates) per day, mostly from non-starchy vegetables, avocados, and nuts. Everyone tolerates a slightly different carbohydrate level, and you'll need to try and find out what works best for you.

The suggestion that the "zero-carb" approach leads to a higher level of ketones and enhanced fat loss is misleading because this is not the main reason for weight loss on the ketogenic diet. It's simple: you will eat less because the ketogenic diet has natural appetite-suppressing effects. There is no scientific evidence that high levels of ketones will lead to enhanced fat loss. Typically, a zero or very low-carb approach may be desirable purely for therapeutic purposes rather than fat loss.

Total Carbs or Net Carbs?

Net carbohydrates are total carbohydrates without fiber. There are two types of fiber: soluble and insoluble. While soluble fiber contains calories, insoluble fiber has zero calories and zero effect on blood sugar. Most foods contain both types of fiber, and foods eaten on a ketogenic diet tend to be higher in insoluble fiber (avocados, nuts, leafy greens, etc.). Fiber has little to no effect on blood sugar, and counting net carbs works well for most people seeking to lose weight and those who want to improve their overall health. However, counting total carbs may be a better option for managing a disease, such as cancer, epilepsy, or Alzheimer's, where carbohydrate restriction is more severe.

Although I follow what is known as the "net carb approach," you can use my book even if you use the total carb approach. All of my recipes include a detailed nutritional breakdown, listing both total and net carbs.

SWAP LOW-CARB VEGETABLES FOR STARCHY SIDES

Zucchini Noodles

Use a julienne peeler or a spiralizer to turn the zucchini into thin or wide "noodles." Chop the soft cores and add them to the noodles. Sprinkle the noodles with salt and let them sit for 10 minutes. Use a paper towel to pat them dry. Set aside.

RECOMMENDED SERVING SIZE: 1 small (150 g/5.3 oz) to medium (200 g/7.1 oz) zucchini
CARBS PER 1 SMALL ZUCCHINI: 3.2 g net carbs, 4.7 g total carbs
CARBS PER 1 MEDIUM ZUCCHINI: 4.2 g net carbs, 6.2 g total carbs

Cauli-rice

Wash the cauliflower thoroughly and drain well. Once dry, grate with a hand grater, or place the florets in a food processor with a grating blade and pulse until it looks like rice. A grating blade will make it look closer to real rice. Don't overdo it. It only takes a few more seconds to make purée out of your cauliflower. Place in an airtight container and store for up to 4 days.

Cook your cauli-rice using these methods:

Steaming: Place in a steam pot and cook for 5 to 7 minutes.

Microwaving: Place the processed cauliflower in a microwave-safe bowl and cook on medium-high for 5 to 7 minutes. You won't need any water when cooking in the microwave.

Pan roasting: You can briefly cook the cauli-rice on a pan greased with butter or ghee, or add it directly to the pot with meat or sauce you plan to serve it with. This method adds extra flavor to your cauli-rice!

Oven cooking: Preheat the oven to 400°F (200°C, or gas mark 6). Spread the grated cauli-rice on a baking sheet lined with parchment paper and cook for 12 to 15 minutes, flipping two or three times. This method is great when you want the rice to be as dry as possible.

RECOMMENDED SERVING SIZE: 1 to 1½ cups (120 to 180 g/4.2 to 6.4 oz)
CARBS PER 1 CUP (120 G): 3.6 g net carbs, 6 g total carbs
CARBS PER 1½ CUPS (180 G): 5.4 g net carbs, 9 g total carbs

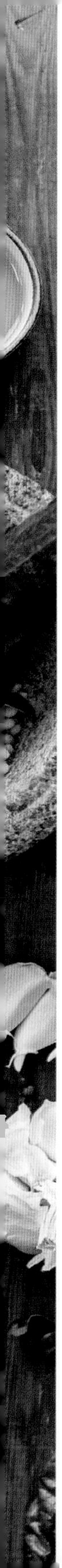

Shirataki Noodles/Rice

Wash the shirataki noodles thoroughly and boil them for 2 to 3 minutes. Drain well. Place the noodles in a hot dry pan. Fry over medium-high heat for about 10 minutes. Using tongs, toss the noodles as they cook. Add the fried noodles directly to a meal, or place in an airtight container and refrigerate for up to 3 days.

RECOMMENDED SERVING SIZE: 3.5 to 5.3 oz (100 to 150 g)
CARBS PER 3.5 OZ (100 G): 1.5 g net carbs, 2.9 g total carbs
CARBS PER 5.3 OZ (150 G): 2.3 g net carbs, 4.4 g total carbs

Spaghetti Squash

Preheat the slow cooker and fill with ½ cup (120 ml) of water. Prick the spaghetti squash several times so that the steam can escape while cooking. Place in the slow cooker and cook on low for 4 hours for average-sized squash, or up to 6 hours for large. When done, remove the squash from the slow cooker. Leave it to cool on a cutting board for 20 minutes, then cut it in half lengthwise or widthwise (this will result in longer strands). Spoon out the seeds and discard. Using a fork, pull the strands out and place them in a bowl.

Cooked spaghetti squash can be stored in the fridge in an airtight container for up to 5 days. For longer storage, divide it into manageable portions and place it in plastic bags, flatten, and freeze flat. The frozen squash will keep for up to 6 months. When ready to serve, let the prepared squash defrost at room temperature or in the fridge.

RECOMMENDED SERVING SIZE: ¾ to 1 cup (116 to 155 g/4.1 to 5.5 oz) cooked spaghetti squash
CARBS PER ¾ CUP (116 G): 5.8 g net carbs, 7.5 g total carbs
CARBS PER 1 CUP (155 G): 7.8 g net carbs, 10 g total carbs

When Should You Buy Organic?

Not all fruits and vegetables need to be labeled organic to be safe to eat. So which ones are worth paying for? Simple! If it's on the Dirty Dozen list (www.ewg.org), always buy organic.

OVERVIEW OF LOW-CARB VEGETABLES

Here are some more healthy veggies that you can use as sides (avocados are technically a fruit, but are included here as they're a staple of the ketodiet). All information is per raw vegetables.

FOOD	SERVING SIZE	TOTAL CARBS (G)	NET CARBS (G)
Arugula	2 cups (20 g/0.7 oz)	0.7	0.4
Asparagus	1 small bunch (150 g/5.3 oz)	5.8	2.7
Avocado	medium-size (150 g/5.3 oz)	12.8	2.7
Bean sprouts	1 cup (50 g/1.8 oz)	3.0	2.0
Broccoli, raw, chopped	1½ cups (137 g/4.8 oz)	9.1	5.5
Brussels sprouts, halved	1¼ cups (110 g/3.9 oz)	9.8	5.7
Cabbage, green, chopped	1½ cups (135 g/4.8 oz)	7.7	4.3
Cabbage, red, chopped	1½ cups (135 g/4.8 oz)	9.9	7.1
Cabbage, white, chopped	1½ cups (135 g/4.8 oz)	7.7	4.4
Cauliflower, chopped	1½ cups (161 g/5.7 oz)	8.0	4.8
Celery stalk	2 large (128 g/4.5 oz)	3.8	1.8
Celeriac (celery root), diced	½ cup (78 g/2.8 oz)	7.2	5.8
Cucumber	1 small (150 g/5.3 oz)	3.2	2.2
Endive	1 small (150 g/5.3 oz)	5.0	0.4
Eggplant	½ medium (150 g/5.3 oz)	8.8	4.3
Fennel, sliced	1½ cups (131 g/4.6 oz)	9.5	5.5
Kale, curly	2 cups (100 g/3.5 oz)	5.6	3.6
Kale, dark cavolo nero	2 cups (100 g/3.5 oz)	4.5	1.4
Kohlrabi, diced	1 cup (135 g/4.8 oz)	8.4	3.5
Lettuce, iceberg, shredded	2 cups (144 g/5.1 oz)	4.3	2.5
Lettuce, Little Gem, shredded	2 cups (144 g/5.1 oz)	3.6	2.2
Lettuce, radicchio, shredded	3 cups (120 g/4.2 oz)	5.4	4.3
Lettuce, romaine, shredded	3 cups (141 g/5 oz)	4.6	1.7
Okra, chopped	1 cup (100 g/3.5 oz)	7.5	4.3
Radishes, sliced	1 cup (116 g/4.1 oz)	3.9	2.1
Rutabaga	¾ cup (105 g/3.7 oz)	9.1	6.6
Spinach	4 cups (120 g/4.2 oz)	4.4	1.7
Swiss chard, chopped	4 cups (144/5.1 oz)	5.4	3.1
Tomatoes	1 medium (123 g/4.3 oz)	4.8	3.2
Turnips, diced	1 cup (130 g/4.6 oz)	8.4	6.0
Watercress, chopped	3 cups (102 g/3.6 oz)	1.3	0.8
Zucchini, chopped	1½ cups (186 g/6.6 oz)	5.8	3.9

Indian Curry Paste Three Ways

Tikka Masala Curry Paste:

4 cloves garlic, peeled
1 small (14 g/0.5 oz) red chile pepper, halved
2½-inch piece (15 g/0.5 oz) ginger root, peeled
1 tablespoon (6 g/0.2 oz) garam masala
1 tablespoon (6 g/0.2 oz) paprika
2 teaspoons ground cumin
2 teaspoons ground coriander
1 teaspoon turmeric powder
½ to 1 teaspoon cayenne pepper
1 teaspoon fine sea salt
1 bunch (30 g/1.1 oz) fresh cilantro, plus more for garnish
2 tablespoons (30 g/1.1 oz) unsweetened tomato paste
¼ cup (63 g/2.2 oz) coconut butter or almond butter
¼ cup (60 ml) water

To prepare curry paste, place all the ingredients in a food processor or a blender. Pulse until smooth. Set aside.

Rogan Josh Curry Paste:

4 cloves garlic, peeled
1 small (14 g/0.5 oz) red chile pepper, halved
2½-inch piece (15 g/0.5 oz) ginger root, peeled
1 tablespoon (6 g/0.2 oz) garam masala
1 tablespoon (6 g/0.2 oz) paprika
2 teaspoons ground cumin
2 teaspoons ground coriander
1 teaspoon turmeric powder
1 teaspoon smoked paprika
½ teaspoon ground cinnamon
½ teaspoon black pepper
1 teaspoon fine sea salt
1 bunch (30 g/1.1 oz) fresh cilantro, plus more for garnish
¼ cup (63 g/2.2 oz) unsweetened tomato paste
3 tablespoons (45 ml) water

To prepare curry paste, place all the ingredients in a food processor or a blender. Pulse until smooth. Set aside.

Korma Curry Paste:

4 cloves garlic, peeled
1 small (14 g/0.5 oz) green chile pepper, halved
2½-inch piece (15 g/0.5 oz) ginger root, peeled
2 teaspoons garam masala
2 teaspoons ground cumin
2 teaspoons ground coriander
½ teaspoon turmeric powder
½ teaspoon ground cinnamon
1 teaspoon fine sea salt
¼ to ½ teaspoon cayenne pepper
1 bunch (30 g/1.1 oz) fresh cilantro, plus more for garnish
2 tablespoons (30 g/1.1 oz) unsweetened tomato paste
¼ cup (60 g/2.1 oz) coconut butter or almond butter
2 tablespoons (30 ml) water

To prepare the curry paste, place all the ingredients in a food processor or a blender and pulse until smooth. Place in an airtight container and refrigerate for up to 1 week, or freeze any remaining curry paste in an ice cube tray for up to 3 months. To enhance the flavor, try toasting whole spices. Instead of ground cumin, coriander, and black pepper, you can use whole seeds and toast them in a hot pan for 1 to 2 minutes before blending into a paste with the remaining ingredients. Although curry paste is usually made with oil, you won't use it in most meals because they already contain other high-fat ingredients (ghee, coconut milk, cream, or coconut butter).

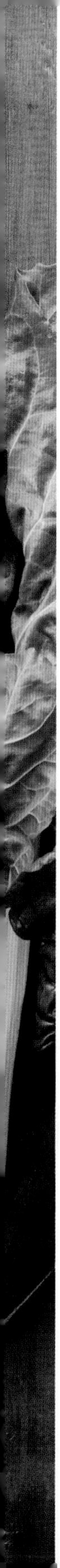

CAN'T FIND HEALTHY ALTERNATIVES? MAKE YOUR OWN!

Quick Mayonnaise

Use a wide-mouth mason jar that just about fits the head of your immersion blender. This is vital for the recipe to work. Place 2 large egg yolks, 2 teaspoons Dijon mustard, 2 tablespoons (30 ml) apple cider vinegar, 2 tablespoons (30 ml) fresh lemon juice, ½ teaspoon fine sea salt, and ¼ teaspoon ground black pepper. Pour 1½ cups (360 ml) walnut oil (or macadamia oil or avocado oil) on top, and let it settle for 20 seconds. Place the head of the immersion blender at the bottom of the jar and turn it on high speed. (Do not pulse.) As the mayonnaise starts to thicken, gently tilt and move the head of the immersion blender until the mayonnaise is thick. Add 2 tablespoons (30 ml/1 oz) whey (the liquid part on top of raw full-fat yogurt), or powder from 1 to 2 probiotic capsules. Cover the jar loosely with a lid or a cloth, and let it sit on a kitchen counter for 8 hours. This is essential in order to activate the enzymes that will keep your mayo fresh. Refrigerate after 8 hours, and use within the next 3 months.

Marinara Sauce

To make a medium jar of marinara sauce (300 g/10.5 oz), you'll need 1 cup (150 g/5.3 oz) cherry tomatoes, ½ cup (20 g/0.7 oz) fresh basil, 2 cloves garlic, 1 small (30 g/1.1 oz) shallot, 4 tablespoons (60 g/2.2 oz) tomato paste, ¼ cup (60 ml) extra-virgin olive oil, ¼ teaspoon salt, and freshly ground pepper to taste. Place all the ingredients in a food processor and blend until smooth. When done, place in an airtight container and store in the fridge for up to 1 week.

Sauerkraut

Sauerkraut (a.k.a. pickled, fermented cabbage) is high in vitamin C and very low in carbs. Sauerkraut is beneficial for your digestive system due to its high levels of probiotics and natural digestive enzymes. To make a 1-quart (950-ml) jar of sauerkraut: Cut 1 large head (1 kg/2.2 lb) cabbage into quarters and remove the hard cores. Discard any dry outer leaves. Slice the cabbage with a knife or use a slicing blade on your food processor. Transfer it to a large bowl; sprinkle with 1 tablespoon (17 g/0.6 oz) salt and optionally with 1 tablespoon (7 g/0.3 oz) caraway seeds, about 10 juniper berries, and/or 1 teaspoon mustard seeds. Mix well and let it sit for about 2 hours.

Press and squeeze the cabbage to release as much of the juices as you can. Place the sweated cabbage in a 1-quart (950-ml) Fido jar, leave a small gap, and close it. Don't worry about the jar exploding; the fermentation gases will escape through the rubber lid while no oxygen will get in, thus there will be no risk of failure. Oxygen is what causes mold, so do not open the jar during fermentation. Keep the jar out of direct sunlight and ferment at room temperature, 60° to 75°F (16° to 24°C), for 3 to 5 weeks. When done, refrigerate, and store for up to 6 months or preserve for longer.

Kimchi

Similar to sauerkraut, kimchi is made through a process called lacto-fermentation and it is good for your gut. To make a 1-quart (950-ml) jar of kimchi: Cut 2 medium (900 g/2 lb) heads of Napa cabbage lengthwise into quarters and remove the cores. Slice each quarter into 1-inch (2.5-cm) strips. Place the sliced cabbage in a large bowl and sprinkle with salt; start with 1 tablespoon (17 g/0.6 oz) and add more if needed. Using your hands, massage the salt into the cabbage to release the juices and soften it. Let the cabbage sit for 20 to 30 minutes.

Once the cabbage has softened, add 6 ounces (170 g) julienned daikon radish, 4 medium (60 g/2.1 oz) sliced spring onions, 4 cloves minced garlic, 2 tablespoons (12 g/0.4 oz) finely chopped fresh ginger, ¼ cup (28 g/1 oz) Korean hot pepper powder, and 1 tablespoon (15 ml) fish sauce. Mix until well combined. (Be sure to wear gloves when handling red pepper flakes.) Optionally, add 2 to 4 tablespoons (20 to 40 g/0.7 to 1.4 oz) of erythritol or Swerve to balance out the spiciness of the chili powder.

Place the vegetables in a sterilized 1-quart (950-ml) Fido jar, pressing down until the brine rises above the vegetables. If there isn't enough juice, add a little salted water until the vegetables are covered. Leave at least 1 inch (2.5 cm) of space between the liquid and the top of the jar, close it, and place on a small tray to catch any juices that may escape during fermentation. Leave the jar in a warm spot in the kitchen to ferment for 3 to 7 days.

The best way to tell whether the kimchi is ready is to taste it during the fermentation process; the longer you leave it, the stronger it'll taste. Once it's done, store in the fridge for up to 6 months. Try it in Korean Beef & Kimchi Stew (page 44).

Cream Cheese

Place 2 cups (480 g) full-fat yogurt into a nut milk bag or cheesecloth, and close the top. Hang on your kitchen counter on a cupboard doorknob over a bowl to collect the whey. You can use the whey to make your mayonnaise stay fresher for longer. Leave to drain for up to 24 hours. When done, store the cream cheese in an airtight container in the fridge for up to 2 weeks. Try it in Chicken Chowder (page 37).

Pumpkin Purée

Preheat the oven to 300°F (150°C, or gas mark 2). Cut the squash in half and place the halves face down on a baking tray lined with parchment paper. Transfer to the oven and bake for 1 to 1½ hours, until soft. Using a fork, pierce the skin to make sure it's cooked. Remove from the oven and let the squash cool down. Using a spoon, remove the seeds, and scoop the pumpkin meat out into a bowl. Place some of the squash in a piece of cheesecloth and squeeze the excess juices out. (You can reuse them in soups and stews.) Repeat for the remaining squash. Place the squash in a blender and process until smooth. Refrigerate for up to 5 days, or freeze for up to 6 months. Try it in Pumpkin Pie Custard (page 83).

Homemade Nut/Seed Milk

Rinse 1 cup of any nuts or seeds (almonds, cashews, hazelnuts, Brazil nuts, hemp seeds; weight will vary). Transfer them to a bowl. Add 3 cups (720 ml) water and leave to soak for 12 to 24 hours. Strain them through a colander and rinse well with water. Discard the water. Place them in a blender and add 3 cups (720 ml) fresh water. Pulse on high speed until smooth.

Use cheesecloth or a nut milk bag and pour the mixture through it. Squeeze out the milk and discard the pulp, or dehydrate it in the oven and store it in an airtight container. Use just like almond meal. You can leave the milk plain or add any spices or low-carb sweeteners of choice (vanilla, cinnamon, stevia, etc.). Pour the milk into a sealable glass bottle and keep in the fridge for up to 4 days.

Coconut Milk versus "Creamed" Coconut Milk

If a recipe calls for coconut milk, you can either use canned coconut milk (solids + liquids), carton coconut milk, or homemade coconut milk (see below).

If a recipe calls for "creamed" coconut milk, you can either buy ready-made coconut cream or make your own using canned coconut milk. Creamed coconut milk is the fatty part of coconut milk that has separated. To cream coconut milk, simply place the can in the fridge overnight. Open it the next day; do not shake before opening the can. Spoon out the solidified coconut milk and discard the liquids. One 13.5 ounce (400 ml) can will yield about 7 ounces (200 grams) of coconut cream.

Homemade Coconut Milk

Place 3 cups (230 g/8 oz) shredded desiccated coconut in a blender, and add 4 to 5 cups (940 ml to 1.2 L) boiling water. Blend on high for 45 to 60 seconds. When done, pour the mixture through a cheesecloth or nut milk bag. Squeeze out the milk and reserve the pulp for future uses. Once the pulp is dry, you can blend it to make fine coconut flour or use it just like desiccated coconut. When the milk is done, add any spices or sweeteners of choice. Pour into a sealable glass bottle. Store in the fridge for up to 2 days and shake well before use.

Homemade Nut, Seed, and Coconut Butter

Place 4 cups (weight will vary) of whole nuts, seeds, or shredded coconut or 5 cups (400 g) flaked coconut in a strong food processor. Process for several minutes, until smooth. Depending on the butter, this will take anywhere between 1 and 8 minutes. High-fat macadamia butter will take about 2 minutes, while coconut butter will take up to 8 minutes. Using a spatula, scrape the butter from the sides several times, as needed. Store at room temperature for up to 1 month.

Homemade Stocks

Stocks are available in most grocery stores, but there is nothing quite like a warming cup of freshly made stock or broth. Both stock and bone broth can be used interchangeably, although they are technically not the same thing. Bone broth (page 33) requires up to ten times longer cooking time and contains higher levels of gelatin. If you're short on time, stock is a great alternative to bone broth. Each of the following recipes will yield 9 to 10 cups (about 2 L) of stock.

Vegetable Stock

2 tablespoons (30 g/1.1 oz) ghee or virgin coconut oil
3 medium (180 g/6.4 oz) carrots, peeled and roughly chopped
4 large (256 g/9 oz) celery stalks, roughly chopped
1 small (150 g/3.5 oz) celeriac, peeled and roughly chopped
1 large (150 g/3.5 oz) yellow onion, halved, skin on
8 cloves garlic, peeled and halved
1 bunch fresh parsley
5 to 6 sprigs thyme
3 bay leaves
1 to 2 teaspoons fine sea salt
Handful of dried porcini mushrooms
2.6 quarts (2.5 L) water

Grease a large saucepan with the ghee. Roast the vegetables and seasonings over medium-high heat for 5 to 10 minutes, stirring frequently. Optionally, add the dried mushrooms, pour in the water, and transfer to a slow cooker. Cook on high for 2 hours or on low for 4 hours. Strain the stock through a muslin-lined sieve into another saucepan and let it cool. Store in the fridge for up to 5 days, or freeze for up to 6 months.

Chicken Stock

3 to 4 pounds (1.4 to 1.8 kg) chicken bones and cartilages (use leftovers from roasts)
1 large (150 g/3.5 oz) yellow onion, halved, skin on
2 medium (120 g/4.2 oz) carrots, peeled and cut into thirds
2 large (128 g/4.5 oz) celery stalks
4 cloves garlic, peeled and halved
3 bay leaves
1 teaspoon whole black peppercorns
2.6 quarts (2.5 L) water

Place all the ingredients in a slow cooker. Cook on high for 4 hours or on low for 8 hours. Strain the stock through a muslin-lined sieve into another saucepan and let it cool. Store in the fridge for up to 4 days, or freeze for up to 3 months.

Seafood/Fish Stock

1½ pounds (680 g) seafood shells (shrimp, lobster, crab), or 3 to 4 pounds (1.4 to 1.8 kg) fish bones and heads
1 large (150 g/3.5 oz) yellow onion, halved, skin on
3 large (192 g/6.8 oz) celery stalks
4 cloves garlic, peeled and halved
2 tablespoons (30 g/1.1 oz) unsweetened tomato paste
2 teaspoons fine sea salt
1 teaspoon whole black peppercorns
2 bay leaves
5 to 6 sprigs fresh thyme
2.6 quarts (2.5 L) water

To enhance the flavor, you can optionally roast the seafood shells in the oven preheated to 400°F (200°C, or gas mark 6) for 10 to 12 minutes. Place all the ingredients in a slow cooker. Cook on high for 2 hours or on low for 4 hours. Strain the stock through a muslin-lined sieve into another saucepan and let it cool. Store in the fridge for up to 3 days, or freeze for up to 3 months.

HERBS AND SPICES ARE YOUR FRIENDS

Herbs and spices will boost flavor while keeping your carbs low. Here are some simple DIY spice blends and curry pastes that will make your keto cooking tasty and effortless.

Cajun Seasoning:

To make about ⅔ cup (95 g) of Cajun seasoning, mix 4 tablespoons (28 g/1 oz) paprika, 2 tablespoons (20 g/0.7 oz) garlic powder, 2 tablespoons (14 g/0.5 oz) onion powder, 2 tablespoons (11 g/0.4 oz) dried oregano, 2 tablespoons (9 g/0.3 oz) dried thyme, 1 tablespoon (7 g/0.3 oz) ground black pepper, and 2 teaspoons cayenne pepper. You can optionally add 1 tablespoon (17 g/0.6 oz) salt or skip and add it directly to the dish. Store in an airtight container for up to 6 months.

Ranch Seasoning:

To make about ⅔ cup (65 g) of ranch seasoning, mix 3 tablespoons (5 g/0.2 oz) dried parsley, 2 tablespoons (4 g/0.2 oz) dried chives, 2 tablespoons (20 g/0.7 oz) garlic powder, 2 tablespoons (14 g/0.5 oz) onion powder, 1 tablespoon (3 g/0.1 oz) dried dill, 1 tablespoon (17 g/0.6 oz) fine sea salt, 1½ teaspoons ground black pepper, and ¾ teaspoon cayenne pepper. Store in an airtight container for up to 6 months.

Pumpkin Pie Spice:

To make about ½ cup (50 g) of pumpkin pie spice, mix 4 tablespoons (31 g/1.1 oz) cinnamon, 2 tablespoons (10 g/0.4 oz) ground ginger, 2 teaspoons ground nutmeg, 1 teaspoon ground cloves, and 1 teaspoon ground allspice. Optionally, add ½ teaspoon ground cardamom and ½ teaspoon ground mace. Store in an airtight container for up to 6 months.

How to Use This Book

When you're sourcing ingredients, try to get them in their most natural forms. That is, organically grown and free from unnecessary additives. Buy organic eggs, organic unwaxed lemons, pastured beef and butter, outdoor-reared pork, wild-caught fish, and extra-virgin coconut oil.

Remember:

- Nutrition values for each recipe are per serving unless stated otherwise. The nutrition data are derived from the USDA National Nutrient Database (ndb.nal.usda.gov).
- Nutrition facts are calculated from edible parts. For example, if one medium green pepper is listed as 120 g/4.2 oz, this value represents its edible parts (seeds and stalk removed) unless otherwise specified.
- Optional ingredients and suggested sides and toppings are not included in the nutrition information.
- All slow cooker recipes have been prepared in a large 6-quart (5.7-L) slow cooker. While most recipes will work in a smaller or larger slow cooker, some recipes will require you to use a large 5- to 6-quart (4.7- to 5.7-L) slow cooker to fit all the ingredients. These recipes always mention that you will need a 5- to 6-quart (4.7- to 5.7-L) slow cooker.
- Recipes that are allergy-free are marked with the appropriate tags:

dairy-free

egg-free

nut-free

vegetarian

Additionally, when a recipe includes an allergy-free option, it is tagged with , , and accordingly.

AN IMPORTANT NOTE ABOUT MEASUREMENTS

If you are following a ketogenic diet for specific health reasons, you should be aware that accuracy is vital in order for this diet to work. When measuring ingredients, always weigh them using a kitchen scale. Using measures like cups or tablespoons can lead to inaccuracies that may affect the macronutrient composition of your meal. All it takes to shift your body out of ketosis is a few extra grams of carbohydrates. Plus, cups and tablespoons for dried products (flax meal, etc.) may vary depending on the brand.

{ Chapter 2 }

HOMEMADE BASICS & STAPLES

If you could see my fridge and freezer, you would always find condiments and basic ingredients I use regularly. And there is a good reason for it—I make most of them myself. They are easy to prepare and budget-friendly, and I never have to worry about added sugar, gluten, and other unwanted ingredients. Still not convinced? Even if you can find "clean" products, chances are they will cost three times more than homemade.

This chapter features my favorite keto staples that I use in recipes throughout this book, from easy-to-make keto condiments, such as pesto, BBQ sauce, and curry paste, to low-carb sides, including creamy cauli-mash, rustic sourdough bread, and even tortillas. These recipes go hand in hand with the stews, roasts, and casseroles!

MAKES: 470 g/16.6 oz
PREPARATION TIME: 5 minutes
COOKING TIME: 5 minutes

Red Pesto

I use homemade pesto almost every day, so I always keep a jar on hand in the fridge. It takes just a few minutes to prepare, and adds zing to everything from casseroles to soups to salads.

Ingredients

- ¼ cup (25 g/0.9 oz) pitted green or black olives
- ½ cup (67 g/2.4 oz) macadamia nuts
- 2 tablespoons (20 g/0.7 oz) pine nuts
- 1 cup (110 g/3.9 oz) sun-dried tomatoes, drained
- 6 cloves garlic, peeled and sliced
- 1 tablespoon (15 ml) fresh lemon juice or apple cider vinegar
- ¼ cup (63 g/2.2 oz) unsweetened tomato paste
- 2 cups (30 g/1.1 oz) fresh basil leaves
- ½ cup (120 ml) extra-virgin olive oil
- ¼ teaspoon fine sea salt
- ¼ teaspoon black pepper
- Optional: ½ cup (45 g/1.6 oz) grated Parmesan cheese

Instructions

Place all the ingredients in a food processor and pulse until smooth. Alternatively, use a mortar and pestle to crush all the ingredients into a smooth paste. Transfer to a jar and refrigerate. You can keep your pesto in the fridge for up to 1 week or two if it's stored properly. It helps to pour a thin layer of olive oil on the top, as it keeps it fresh longer. Whenever you use the pesto, remember to add another thin layer of olive oil before you put it back in the fridge.

TIP: If you want to make this pesto nut-free, instead of macadamia nuts and pine nuts, use an equal amount of sunflower seeds. It's better if you use soaked and dehydrated nuts or seeds.

To preserve pesto for longer, spoon it into an ice cube tray and place in the freezer. Once frozen, empty the ice cube tray into a resealable plastic bag. Keep your frozen pesto cubes for up to 6 months.

NUTRITION FACTS PER TABLESPOON (15 G/0.5 OZ):
Total carbs: 1.6 g / Fiber: 0.5 g / Net carbs: 1.1 g / Protein: 0.5 g / Fat: 6.1 g / Energy: 61 kcal
Macronutrient ratio: Calories from carbs (7%), protein (4%), fat (89%)

MAKES: 550 g/1.2 lb
PREPARATION TIME: 20 minutes
COOKING TIME: 40 minutes

Harissa Paste

Made from red peppers, chiles, and spices, this North African paste is so versatile. I use it as a meat marinade, with cauli-rice, and mixed with full-fat yogurt as a keto-friendly salad dressing. Use a combination of your favorite chiles, and adjust the amount of harissa you use in your recipes according to its heat.

Ingredients

HARISSA PASTE:

2 medium (240 g/8.5 oz) red peppers
5 ounces (140 g) dried chiles of choice (any combination of guajillo, New Mexico, ancho, chipotle, arbol)
4 to 6 pieces (28 g/1 oz) sun-dried tomatoes, drained
6 cloves garlic, peeled
1 teaspoon ground turmeric
2 teaspoons fine sea salt
¼ cup (60 ml) extra-virgin olive oil
Juice from 1 lemon (about 60 ml/¼ cup)

SPICES FOR TOASTING:

1 teaspoon whole coriander seeds
1 teaspoon whole cumin seeds
1 teaspoon whole caraway seeds

Instructions

Roast the bell peppers in an oven preheated to 350°F (175°C, or gas mark 4). Bake for 30 to 40 minutes, or until the skin is charred and the peppers are soft. Remove from the oven. Put a piece of baking foil over the peppers and set aside to cool until they are easy to handle. Peel the skin and remove the seeds.

While the peppers are baking, place the dried chiles in a pot and cover with 2 cups (480 ml) boiling water. Cover with a lid and let them sit for 20 to 30 minutes. Drain the chiles, and discard the stems and seeds.

Place the coriander, cumin, and caraway seeds in a hot pan and dry-roast briefly for just a minute or two. Grind the spices in a mortar and pestle or a coffee grinder.

Place all ingredients in a food processor or blender: chiles, bell peppers, toasted spices, sun-dried tomatoes, garlic, turmeric, salt, olive oil, and lemon juice. Process until smooth, spoon into a jar, and store in the fridge for up to 1 week. To preserve harissa for longer, spoon it into an ice cube tray and place in the freezer. Once frozen, empty the ice cube tray into a resealable plastic bag. Keep your frozen harissa cubes for up to 6 months.

TIP: Use a combination of your favorite chiles. A combination of fresh, sweet, bell peppers with guajillo, ancho, and chipotle chiles results in moderate-mild spicy harissa. If you prefer more heat, add some arbol chiles or skip the bell peppers. Don't forget to adjust the amount of harissa used in recipes to adjust for the heat.

NUTRITION FACTS PER TABLESPOON (15 G/0.5 OZ):
Total carbs: 2.9 g / Fiber: 1.1 g / Net carbs: 1.8 g / Protein: 0.3 g / Fat: 2 g / Energy: 29 kcal
Macronutrient ratio: Calories from carbs (27%), protein (9%), fat (64%)

MAKES: about 4 cups (900 g/2 lb)
PREPARATION TIME: 15 minutes
COOKING TIME: 6 hours

Sweet & Sour BBQ Sauce

This sweet, tangy, easy-to-prepare BBQ sauce is the perfect way to dress up juicy ribs, fork-tender pulled pork, and comforting meat stews.

Ingredients

- 2 tablespoons (30 g/1.1 oz) ghee or other healthy cooking fat
- 1 large (150 g/5.3 oz) yellow onion, peeled and diced
- 4 cloves garlic, peeled and minced
- 2 pieces (28 g/1 oz) jalapeño peppers, seeds and core removed
- 1½ cups (360 g/12.7 oz) canned tomatoes
- ½ cup (125 g/4.4 oz) unsweetened tomato paste
- ½ cup (120 ml) apple cider vinegar or coconut vinegar
- ¼ cup (60 ml) coconut aminos
- ¼ cup (50 g/1.8 oz) granulated erythritol or Swerve
- 2 teaspoons paprika, sweet or smoked
- 2 teaspoons mustard powder
- 1 teaspoon celery seeds
- ½ teaspoon chili powder
- ½ teaspoon black pepper
- ⅛ teaspoon ground cloves
- ⅛ teaspoon ground allspice
- 1 teaspoon fine sea salt, or to taste
- 2 teaspoons extra-virgin olive oil
- Optional: few drops of liquid stevia

Instructions

Preheat your slow cooker to low. In a pan greased with ghee, cook the onion over medium-low heat for about 10 minutes, until browned and fragrant. Add the garlic and cook for another minute.

Place the browned onion and garlic in the preheated slow cooker. Add all the remaining ingredients, apart from the olive oil, and cook for 6 hours. When done, turn off the heat and let it cool for an hour. Add the olive oil. Using a blender, process the sauce until smooth. Transfer to a glass jar and keep in the fridge for up to a month. For longer storage, spoon the sauce into an ice cube tray and freeze for 2 hours. Place in a bag and store in the freezer for up to 6 months.

NUTRITION FACTS PER TABLESPOON (15 G/0.5 OZ):
Total carbs: 1 g / Fiber: 0.2 g / Net carbs: 0.8 g / Protein: 0.2 g /Fat: 1 g / Energy: 13 kcal
Macronutrient ratio: Calories from carbs (23%), protein (5%), fat (72%)

MAKES: about 4 cups (900 g/2 lb)
PREPARATION TIME: 5 minutes
COOKING TIME: 4 hours

Cranberry Sauce

This spiced, sugar-free cranberry sauce is an all-rounder: it works well in both sweet and savory recipes. Try serving it alongside roast turkey at the holidays; mix it into full-fat yogurt as a snack; or use it as a cheesecake topping.

Ingredients

- **1.3 pounds (600 g) cranberries, fresh or frozen**
- **Juice and zest from 1 medium (150 g/5.3 oz) orange**
- **1 cup (240 ml) water**
- **⅔ cup (133 g/4.7 oz) granulated erythritol or Swerve**
- **20 to 30 drops liquid stevia**
- **1 teaspoon ground cinnamon or 2 to 3 cinnamon sticks**
- **½ teaspoon vanilla powder or 2 teaspoons unsweetened vanilla extract**
- **½ teaspoon ginger powder**
- **¼ teaspoon ground cloves**

Instructions

Preheat your slow cooker to high. Place all the ingredients in the slow cooker, cover with a lid, and cook for 3½ hours. Remove the lid and mix. Cook uncovered for another 30 minutes. When done, mix, let it cool, and place it in jars. Store in the fridge for up to 2 weeks. For longer storage, spoon into an ice cube tray and freeze for 2 to 3 hours. Place in a bag and freeze for up to 6 months.

TIPS: A small amount of orange juice will have no significant effect on carbs per serving. If you prefer to avoid it, you can use ¼ cup (60 ml) lemon or lime juice instead.

For a richer flavor, you can substitute ½ cup (120 ml) water with ½ cup (120 ml) of dry red wine.

If you don't like your sauce chunky, spoon it into a blender and pulse until smooth.

NUTRITION FACTS PER TABLESPOON (20 G/0.7 OZ):
Total carbs: 2.1 g / Fiber: 0.6 g / Net carbs: 1.5 g / Protein: 0.1 g / Fat: 0 g / Energy: 8 kcal
Macronutrient ratio: Calories from carbs (92%), protein (5%), fat (3%)

MAKES: 10 tortillas
PREPARATION TIME: 20 minutes
COOKING TIME: 20 minutes + chilling

Keto Tortillas Three Ways

These tortillas are based on one of the most popular recipes on my blog, and with good reason: they're just like the real thing! Soft and flexible, they're ideal with pulled pork, roasted vegetables, and avocado slices.

Ingredients

BASIC INGREDIENTS:

1 cup (100 g/3.5 oz) almond flour
¾ cup (113 g/4 oz) flax meal
¼ cup (30 g/1.1 oz) coconut flour
2 tablespoons (8 g/0.3 oz) whole psyllium husks
2 tablespoons (15 g/0.5 oz) ground chia seeds
1 teaspoon fine sea salt
2 tablespoons (30 g/1.1 oz) ghee or other healthy cooking fat

FOR SPINACH TORTILLAS:

2 cups (312 g/11 oz) frozen spinach, thawed, drained, and puréed
1 teaspoon ground cumin
¾ cup (180 ml) lukewarm water, plus a few tablespoons if the dough is too dry

FOR PESTO TORTILLAS:

3 tablespoons (45 g/1.6 oz) Red Pesto (page 26)
½ cup (45 g/1.6 oz) grated Parmesan
1 cup (240 ml) lukewarm water, plus a few tablespoons if the dough is too dry

Instructions

Combine all the basic ingredients, apart from the cooking fat. Add all the other ingredients needed to make spinach, pesto, or curried tortillas. (If making spinach tortillas, drain the frozen spinach and discard the excess water. Place in a blender and process until puréed.) If the dough is too dry to roll, add a few more tablespoons of water. Mix well using your hands and shape into an oval. Let the dough rest in the fridge for up to 1 hour.

When ready, remove the dough from the fridge and cut it into 6 equal pieces. (You will make the remaining 4 tortillas using the excess dough.) Place a piece of the dough between 2 pieces of parchment paper and roll it out until very thin. Alternatively, use a silicone roller and a silicone mat.

Remove the top parchment paper. Press a large 8-inch (20-cm) lid into the dough (or use a piece of parchment paper to cut into a round shape). Trace around it with your knife to cut out the tortilla.

Repeat for the remaining pieces of dough. Add the cut-off excess dough to the last piece and create the remaining 4 tortillas from it. If you have any dough left over, simply roll it out and cut it into tortilla-chip shapes.

Grease a large pan with ghee and cook 1 tortilla at a time for 2 to 3 minutes on each side over medium heat until lightly browned. Don't overcook it: it'll become too crispy. Once cool, store the tortillas in an airtight container for up to 1 week and reheat them in a dry pan, if needed.

FOR CURRIED TORTILLAS:

2 tablespoons (30 g/1.1 oz) curry paste (pages 17–18)

1 cup (240 ml) lukewarm water, plus a few tablespoons if the dough is too dry

Tip: It works with Harissa Paste (page 27) too!

TIP: To make taco shells, cut small pieces of parchment paper and place the tortillas on top. Fold over a rack in the oven and turn the oven on. Make sure you make them wide enough so you can fit the filling in later. Cook until the oven reaches 400°F (200°C, or gas mark 6) and then cook for 5 to 8 minutes, or until crispy.

NUTRITION FACTS PER TORTILLA (SPINACH/PESTO/CURRIED):
Total carbs: 8.7/7.9/7.8 g / Fiber: 6.7/5.9/5.8 g / Net carbs: 2/2/2 g / Protein: 6.2/6.8/5.1 g
Fat: 14.2/17/14 g / Energy: 176/202/168 kcal
Macronutrient ratio: Calories from carbs (5/4/5%), protein (15/15/13%), fat (80/81/82%)

MAKES: 12 servings
PREPARATION TIME: 20 minutes
COOKING TIME: 3 to 4 hours

Make-Ahead Slow Cooker Mash

Laden with fresh herbs, slow-cooker cauliflower mash is the perfect side for your stews and casseroles. It freezes well, too, so go ahead and make a big batch. For a super-creamy version, add 1 cup (240 g/8.5 oz) cream cheese or sour cream just before blending.

Ingredients

2 to 3 heads (2 kg/4.4 lb) cauliflower, cut into florets
8 cups (1.9 L) water, or enough to cover the cauliflower
2 teaspoons fine sea salt, plus more to taste
1 teaspoon whole peppercorns
2 bay leaves
3 whole allspice
½ cup (110 g/3.9 oz) ghee or other healthy cooking fat
1 large (150 g/5.3 oz) yellow onion, sliced
4 cloves garlic, minced
¼ cup (15 g/0.5 oz) freshly chopped herbs of choice (parsley, dill, thyme, rosemary, etc.)

Instructions

Preheat a 5- to 6-quart (4.7- to 5.7-L) slow cooker. Place the cauliflower florets, water, salt, peppercorns, bay leaves, and allspice in the slow cooker (use a spice bag to easily remove the spices). Cover with a lid. Cook on high for 3 to 4 hours or on low for 6 to 8 hours.

Grease a skillet with the ghee. Add the onion and cook over medium-high heat for about 10 minutes, or until golden brown. Add the garlic and cook for another minute. When done, take off the heat and set aside.

When the cauliflower is tender, turn the slow cooker off and drain the water by pouring it through a colander. Discard the spices. Place the cauliflower back in the slow cooker and process with an immersion blender for a chunky texture. Or purée in batches in a food processor for a creamy texture. Add the cooked onion and garlic, including the ghee, and process to combine. Taste and season with more salt and pepper if needed. Add the fresh herbs and stir in until combined.

Eat as a side with meat, or let it cool down and store in an airtight container for up to 5 days. To store for longer, spoon into single- or double-serving freezer bags.

NUTRITION FACTS PER SERVING (ABOUT ¾ CUP/180 G/6.4 OZ):
Total carbs: 9.8 g / Fiber: 3.7 g / Net carbs: 6.1 g / Protein: 3.4 g / Fat: 9.7 g / Energy: 131 kcal
Macronutrient ratio: Calories from carbs (20%), protein (11%), fat (69%)

MAKES: 6 to 8 cups
PREPARATION TIME: 10 minutes
COOKING TIME: 2 hours or more

Bone Broth

Homemade bone broth is both tasty and high in healthy gelatin and minerals. (And it's great for keeping keto-flu at bay, too!) Give your Bone Broth an antioxidant and anti-inflammatory boost by adding a little turmeric to the mix.

Ingredients

- 2 medium (120 g/4.2 oz) carrots, peeled and cut into thirds
- 1 large (150 g/5.3 oz) white onion, halved
- 4 to 6 cloves garlic, halved
- 2 large (128 g/4.5 oz) celery stalks, cut into thirds
- 3.3 pounds (1.5 kg) oxtail or assorted bones (chicken feet, marrowbones, etc.)
- 2 tablespoons (30 ml/1 fl oz) apple cider vinegar or lemon juice
- 3 bay leaves
- 3 whole allspice
- 1 tablespoon (17 g/0.6 oz) fine sea salt
- 2-inch (5 cm) piece turmeric, sliced, or 1 teaspoon turmeric powder
- 8 to 10 cups (1.9 to 2.4 L/64 to 81 fl oz) water (enough to cover the bones, no more than ⅔ the capacity of the pressure cooker, ¾ of the Dutch oven, or ¾ of the slow cooker)

Instructions

Place all the ingredients in the slow cooker. Cover with a lid. Cook on high for 4 to 5 hours or on low for 8 to 10 hours. Remove the oxtail using tongs and shred the meat using a fork (use the cooked meat for quick meals). Place the bones back in the slow cooker and cook on low for up to 48 hours (optional but highly recommended). Once the broth has cooled, strain it through a sieve, and store it without any bones, spices, or vegetables. Keep it in the fridge if you're planning to use it over the next 4 to 5 days. For future uses, store it in small containers and freeze.

TIP: Oxtail is high in fat, and the greasy layer on top—the tallow—will solidify. Simply scrape most of the tallow off and discard or reuse it for cooking.

NUTRITION FACTS PER CUP (240 ML):
Total carbs: 0.9 g / Fiber: 0.2 g / Net carbs: 0.7 g / Protein: 3.6 g / Fat: 6 g / Energy: 72 kcal
Macronutrient ratio: Calories from carbs (4%), protein (20%), fat (76%)
Note: Nutrition facts, especially protein, in homemade bone broth vary and depend on several factors, such as type of bones used and cooking time.

MAKES: 8 regular or 16 mini buns
PREPARATION TIME: 15 minutes
COOKING TIME: 40 to 45 minutes

Sourdough Keto Buns

This is the absolute best bread recipe I've ever come across—low-carb or otherwise! These buns are fluffy and flavorful, and taste just like the loaves of rustic bread my grandma used to make.

Ingredients

DRY INGREDIENTS:

1½ cups (150 g/5.3 oz) almond flour
⅓ cup (40 g/1.4 oz) psyllium husk powder
½ cup (60 g/2.1 oz) coconut flour
½ cup (75 g/2.6 oz) flax meal
1 teaspoon baking soda
1 teaspoon fine sea salt

WET INGREDIENTS:

6 large egg whites
2 large eggs
¾ cup (180 g/6.5 oz) low-fat buttermilk (see tips)
¼ cup (60 ml) apple cider vinegar
1 cup (240 ml) lukewarm water

Instructions

Preheat the oven to 350°F (180°C, or gas mark 4). Mix all the dry ingredients in a bowl. In a separate bowl, mix the egg whites, eggs, and buttermilk. Add the egg mixture to the dry mixture, and process well using a mixer until the dough is thick. Add the vinegar and lukewarm water, and process until well combined. Do not overprocess the dough. Using a spoon, make 8 regular or 16 mini buns. Place them on a baking tray lined with parchment paper or a nonstick mat, leaving some space between them.

Transfer them to the oven and bake for 10 minutes. Reduce the temperature to 300°F (150°C, or gas mark 2) and bake for another 30 to 45 minutes (small buns will take less time to cook). Remove from the oven, let them cool, and place the buns on a rack to cool to room temperature. Store them at room temperature if you plan to use them in the next couple of days or store in the freezer for up to 3 months.

NUTRITION FACTS PER MINI BUN:
Total carbs: 7 g / Fiber: 4.8 g / Net carbs: 2.2 g / Protein: 6.1 g / Fat: 8.2 g / Energy: 116 kcal
Macronutrient ratio: Calories from carbs (8%), protein (23%), fat (69%)

MAKES: 4 servings
PREPARATION TIME: 15 minutes
COOKING TIME: 5 minutes

Cauliflower Rice Three Ways

Skip the starchy sides and make keto-friendly (and vitamin-C-rich) cauliflower rice instead: it's the perfect partner for slow-cooked meat and flavorful sauces. Just add your favorite spices and you're good to go!

Ingredients

1 medium (720 g/1.6 lb) cauliflower
2 tablespoons (30 g/1.1 oz) ghee or other healthy cooking fat
Salt and freshly ground black pepper

MASALA CAULI-RICE:

1 teaspoon garam masala
½ teaspoon onion powder
¼ teaspoon turmeric powder
⅛ teaspoon chili powder

LEMON & HERB CAULI-RICE:

2 tablespoons (8 g/0.3 oz) fresh herbs such as basil, oregano, thyme, and parsley
1 teaspoon fresh lemon zest
½ teaspoon garlic powder

SPANISH CAULI-RICE:

½ teaspoon onion powder
½ teaspoon garlic powder
2 tablespoons (30 g/1.1 oz) tomato paste

Instructions

Run the cauliflower florets through a hand grater or food processor with a grating blade. Pulse until the florets resemble grains of rice.

Grease a large saucepan with ghee and add all the aromatics for the preferred cauli-rice recipe: Masala, Lemon & Herb, or Spanish. Mix and cook over medium-low heat for up to 1 minute. Add the cauliflower rice and cook for 5 to 7 minutes, stirring constantly. Season with salt and pepper, and serve with slow-cooked meat and sauce. To store, let it cool and place in an airtight container. Refrigerate for up to 5 days.

NUTRITION FACTS PER SERVING (ABOUT 1 CUP MASALA/LEMON & HERB/SPANISH CAULI-RICE):
Total carbs: 9.6/9.4/10.2 g / Fiber: 3.8/3.7/3.9 g / Net carbs: 5.8/5.7/6.3 g / Protein: 3.6/3.6/3.7 g
Fat: 8.1/8/8 g / Energy: 116/115/118 kcal
Macronutrient ratio: Calories from carbs (21/21/23%), protein (13/13/13%), fat (66/66/64%)

{ Chapter 3 }

SATISFYING & NOURISHING SOUPS & STEWS

There is nothing more comforting than a hot bowl of hearty soup or stew on a chilly, rainy day. And soups are not just for winter! Recipes included in this chapter can be enjoyed throughout the year. They are easy, simple, and perfect for feeding hungry crowds. They are also nutritious enough to be enjoyed as complete meals.

MAKES: 8 servings
PREPARATION TIME: 20 minutes
COOKING TIME: 3 to 4 hours

Chicken Chowder

This family-friendly chicken chowder is incredibly creamy and sating, since it's full of protein and healthy fats. And since you can do most of the prep the night before, it makes an ideal weeknight dinner.

Ingredients

- 2 tablespoons (30 g/1.1 oz) duck fat or other healthy cooking fat
- 1 medium (110 g/3.9 oz) yellow onion, sliced
- 1.3 pounds (600 g) skinless chicken thighs, cubed
- 1 teaspoon fine sea salt, or to taste
- ½ teaspoon white or black pepper
- 1 medium (80 g/2.8 oz) carrot, peeled and sliced
- 2 large (128 g/4.5 oz) celery stalks, sliced
- 3 cloves garlic, minced
- 2 cups (200 g/7.1 oz) green beans, trimmed and cut into thirds
- 2 medium (400 g/14.1 oz) turnips, peeled and cut into 1-inch (2.5-cm) pieces
- 2 bay leaves
- 1 teaspoon dried thyme
- 1 teaspoon oregano
- 1 cup (240 g/8.5 oz) full-fat cream cheese
- 3 cups (720 ml) chicken stock (page 22) or bone broth (page 33)
- 2 cups (480 ml) water
- 1½ cups (360 ml) heavy whipping cream
- 6 large (180 g/6.3 oz) slices bacon, crisped up and crumbled
- Fresh parsley or chives for garnish

Instructions

Preheat the slow cooker. In a large heavy-based saucepan greased with ghee, cook the onion over medium-high heat for 5 to 8 minutes, until lightly browned. Add the chicken and cook until browned on all sides, 1 to 2 minutes, stirring frequently. Season with salt and pepper, and transfer to the slow cooker.

Add the carrot, celery, garlic, green beans, turnips, bay leaves, thyme, oregano, cream cheese, chicken stock, and water. Cook on high for 3 to 4 hours or on low for 6 to 8 hours. Add the cream in the last 30 minutes of the cooking process. Discard the bay leaves. To serve, pour into serving bowls, and top with bacon and garnish with fresh herbs. To store, let it cool, and refrigerate in an airtight container for up to 4 days or freeze for up to 3 months.

NUTRITION FACTS PER SERVING (ABOUT 1½ CUPS/360 ML):
Total carbs: 10.5 g / Fiber: 2.7 g / Net carbs: 7.8 g / Protein: 23.6 g / Fat: 40 g / Energy: 485 kcal
Macronutrient ratio: Calories from carbs (6%), protein (19%), fat (75%)

MAKES: 8 servings
PREPARATION TIME: 10 minutes
COOKING TIME: 2 to 3 hours

Broccoli Cheese Soup

Cheesy, creamy, and filling, this simple, starch-free soup is even better than the traditional version. And you won't miss the flour one bit: blending fresh vegetables with Cheddar cheese ensures a deliciously thick and silky result.

Ingredients

1 medium (300 g/10.6 oz) broccoli
½ medium (300 g/10.6 oz) cauliflower
2 tablespoons (30 g/1.1 oz) ghee or other healthy cooking fat
1 medium (110 g/3.9 oz) yellow onion, chopped
2 cloves garlic, minced
1 medium (85 g/3 oz) leek, sliced
2 large (128 g/4.5 oz) celery stalks, sliced
4 cups (1.2 L) vegetable stock or chicken stock (page 22)
3 cups (720 ml) water
1 cup (240 ml) heavy whipping cream
2 cups (226 g/8 oz) shredded Cheddar cheese
2 tablespoons (8 g/0.3 oz) freshly chopped parsley, plus more for garnish
Salt and pepper

Instructions

Preheat a 5- to 6-quart (4.7- to 5.7-L) slow cooker. Cut the broccoli and cauliflower into florets. Peel and roughly chop the broccoli stalks. Heat a skillet greased with ghee over medium-high heat. Add the onion and cook for 5 to 8 minutes, until lightly browned, stirring frequently. Add the garlic, leek, and celery. Cook for 1 to 2 minutes.

Place in the slow cooker, and add the cauliflower and broccoli pieces, vegetable stock, and water. Cover with a lid. Cook on high for 2 to 3 hours or on low for 4 to 6 hours.

Slowly pour in the cream while stirring. Add the Cheddar cheese and parsley (keep some cheese and parsley for garnish). Use an immersion blender and process until puréed, smooth or chunky. If using a regular blender, let the soup cool for 15 to 20 minutes (hot liquids can be dangerous!). Season with salt and pepper to taste, and garnish with the reserved cheese and parsley. To store, let it cool, and refrigerate in an airtight container for up to 5 days or freeze for up to 3 months.

NUTRITION FACTS PER SERVING (ABOUT 1½ CUPS/360 ML):
Total carbs: 8.6 g / Fiber: 2.3 g / Net carbs: 6.3 g / Protein: 10.3 g / Fat: 30.2 g / Energy: 344 kcal
Macronutrient ratio: Calories from carbs (7%), protein (12%), fat (81%)

MAKES: 8 servings
PREPARATION TIME: 15 minutes
COOKING TIME: 6 hours + marinating

Moroccan Chicken Stew

Since it's naturally low-carb, harissa paste is a great way to add spicy, smoky flavor to almost any dish—like this stew, which is a close cousin of traditional Moroccan tagine. When you make it in a slow cooker, you'll end up with perfectly tender, flavorful chicken every single time.

Ingredients

2.7 pounds (1.2 kg) boneless and skinless chicken thighs, cut into 1½-inch (4-cm) chunks
½ cup (120 g/4.2 oz) mild Harissa Paste (page 27)
2 tablespoons (30 g/1.1 oz) ghee or other healthy cooking fat
1 small (70 g/2.5 oz) yellow onion, chopped
½ teaspoon ground cinnamon
½ teaspoon ground ginger
½ teaspoon ground cumin
½ teaspoon black pepper
1 teaspoon fine sea salt, or to taste
1½ cups (320 ml) chicken stock (page 22) or bone broth (page 33)
1 cup (240 g/8.5 oz) canned chopped tomatoes
3 tablespoons (45 ml) fresh lemon juice
½ cup (50 g/1.8 oz) pitted green olives, sliced
1 medium (250 g/8.8 oz) eggplant, cut into 1-inch (2.5-cm) pieces
2 cups (235 g/8.3 oz) diced pumpkin, cut into 1-inch (2.5-cm) pieces

Suggested sides: cauli-rice (page 35) or shirataki rice (page 15)
Optional toppings: ½ cup (45 g/1.6 oz) toasted flaked almonds, 1 cup (230 g/8.1 oz) full-fat sour cream, and fresh cilantro

Instructions

Place the chicken chunks in a bowl and cover in the harissa paste. Cover and let it marinate for 30 minutes, or up to 2 hours in the fridge.

Preheat the slow cooker. Grease a large heavy-based saucepan or Dutch oven with the ghee. Add the onion and cook over medium-high heat for 5 to 8 minutes, until lightly browned. Add the marinated chicken, cinnamon, ginger, cumin, black pepper, and salt. Cook for 2 to 3 minutes, stirring frequently. Add the chicken stock and heat through. Transfer to the slow cooker and add the tomatoes, lemon juice, olives, eggplant, and pumpkin.

Cover with a lid, and cook on low for 6 hours or on high for 3 hours. When done, taste and season if needed. Serve with steamed cauli-rice or shirataki rice. Optionally, top with toasted flaked almonds, sour cream, and cilantro. To store, let it cool, and refrigerate for up to 4 days or freeze for up to 3 months.

NUTRITION FACTS PER SERVING:
Total carbs: 9.6 g / Fiber: 3.1 g / Net carbs: 6.5 g / Protein: 23.7 g / Fat: 50.9 g / Energy: 589 kcal
Macronutrient ratio: Calories from carbs (4%), protein (16%), fat (80%)

MAKES: 6 servings
PREPARATION TIME: 20 minutes
COOKING TIME: 4 hours

Caribbean Beef Stew

There's nothing boring about this hearty Jamaican-style beef stew. Garlic, ginger, chile, and allspice put a spring in its step, and it's full of low-carb vegetables, too. Try it over Cauli-Rice, or with a mess of leafy greens.

Ingredients

- 2 pounds (900 g) beef chuck steak
- ¾ teaspoon fine sea salt, or to taste
- Ground black pepper
- 2 tablespoons (30 g/1.1 oz) ghee or other healthy cooking fat, divided
- 1 small (70 g/2.5 oz) yellow onion, chopped
- 2 cloves garlic, minced
- 1-inch piece (6 g/0.2 oz) ginger, finely chopped
- 1 small (14 g/0.5 oz) red chile pepper, chopped
- 2 cups (480 ml) bone broth (page 33) or water
- 1 cup (240 g/8.5 oz) canned diced tomatoes
- 2 tablespoons (30 ml) coconut aminos
- 1 tablespoon (7 g/0.2 oz) paprika
- 2 bay leaves
- ¼ teaspoon allspice
- 1 medium (120 g/4.2 oz) red bell pepper, sliced
- 1½ cups (174 g/6.1 oz) diced pumpkin
- 1 medium (200 g/7.1 oz) zucchini, diced
- 2 tablespoons (8 g/0.3 oz) freshly chopped cilantro, parsley, or spring onion for garnish
- Suggested side: cauli-rice (page 35) or shirataki rice (page 15)

Instructions

Preheat the slow cooker. Cut the beef into large (about 1½-inch/4-cm) chunks, and season with salt and pepper. To brown the beef, grease a large heavy-based saucepan or Dutch oven with half of the ghee. Cook the beef in batches until browned on all sides and transfer to the slow cooker.

Grease the saucepan with the remaining ghee. Add the onion and cook over medium-high heat for 5 to 8 minutes, until lightly browned. Add the garlic, ginger, and chile pepper, and cook for 1 to 2 minutes. Pour in the bone broth to deglaze the saucepan, scraping the browned bits off the bottom. Pour into the slow cooker over the browned beef. Add the tomatoes, coconut aminos, paprika, bay leaves, and allspice. Combine with a spatula, cover with a lid, and cook on high for 4 hours.

After 2 hours of cooking, mix in the red pepper, pumpkin, and zucchini. Cover with a lid and cook for another 2 hours. Garnish with fresh herbs, and serve with cauli-rice (page 35). To store, let it cool, and refrigerate for up to 4 days or freeze for up to 3 months.

NUTRITION FACTS PER SERVING:
Total carbs: 8.6 g / Fiber: 2 g / Net carbs: 6.6 g / Protein: 31.7 g / Fat: 33.4 g / Energy: 464 kcal
Macronutrient ratio: Calories from carbs (6%), protein (28%), fat (66%)

MAKES: 10 servings
PREPARATION TIME: 20 minutes
COOKING TIME: 5½ hours

Autumn Beef & Vegetable Stew

When the weather turns colder, we reach for woolly sweaters, autumn spices, and plenty of comfort food, like this beef stew. It's an all-time slow-cooker favorite in my house, and it's perfectly balanced for a keto diet: it's high in fat, low in carbs, and rich in electrolytes.

Ingredients

- 3.3 pounds (1.5 kg) beef chuck or shin steaks
- 1½ teaspoon fine sea salt, or to taste
- Ground black pepper
- ½ cup (110 g/3.9 oz) ghee or other healthy cooking fat, divided
- 1 medium (110 g/3.9 oz) white onion, chopped
- 4 cloves garlic, minced
- 1 can (400 g/14.1 oz) chopped tomatoes, unsweetened
- 1 cup (240 ml) bone broth (page 33), vegetable stock (page 22), or water
- 2 tablespoons ground cumin
- 1 tablespoon paprika
- 1 teaspoon ground ginger
- 1 teaspoon chili powder
- 1 teaspoon ground coriander
- 1 teaspoon turmeric powder
- 2 cinnamon sticks
- 2 bay leaves
- 1 large (600 g/1.3 lb) rutabaga, peeled and cut into 1-inch (2.5-cm) pieces
- 4 or 5 medium (1 kg/2.2 lb) zucchini or marrow squash, diced
- Fresh parsley or cilantro

Instructions

Preheat a 5- to 6-quart (4.7- to 5.7-L) slow cooker. Using a paper towel, pat dry the beef, and season with salt and pepper on both sides. Place 2 or 3 steaks at a time in a hot pan greased with half of the ghee and sear until lightly browned all over. When done, transfer to the preheated slow cooker.

Grease the saucepan with the remaining ghee. Add the onion and cook over medium-high heat for 5 to 8 minutes, or until lightly browned. Add the garlic, tomatoes, broth, cumin, paprika, ginger, chili powder, coriander, and turmeric. Bring to a boil, and then pour into the slow cooker over the meat. Add the cinnamon sticks and bay leaves. Cover with a lid and cook on high for 5 to 5½ hours.

After the meat has been cooking for 3 hours, use a spatula to push the meat to one side of the slow cooker and add the rutabaga and zucchini next to it. Cover and cook in the juices for another 2 to 2½ hours. The stew is cooked when the rutabaga and zucchini are fork-tender. Discard the bay leaves and cinnamon sticks. Season with more salt and pepper, and serve with fresh herbs. To store, let it cool, and refrigerate for up to 4 days or freeze for up to 3 months.

NUTRITION FACTS PER SERVING:
Total carbs: 12.7 g / Fiber: 3.6 g / Net carbs: 9.1 g / Protein: 31.9 g / Fat: 39.5 g / Energy: 534 kcal
Macronutrient ratio: Calories from carbs (7%), protein (25%), fat (68%)

MAKES: 6 servings
PREPARATION TIME: 15 minutes
COOKING TIME: 4 hours

Korean Beef & Kimchi Stew

If you've never tried kimchi—that is, Korean fermented cabbage—before, this stew is the place to start: kimchi is responsible for its amazing depth of flavor and slow-burning heat. Serve it over cauli-rce (page 35) that's been cooked in the beef's juices. You'll fall in love with it.

Ingredients

STEW:

2 pounds (900 g) beef chuck
½ teaspoon fine sea salt, or to taste
½ teaspoon ground black pepper, plus more for seasoning the beef
3 tablespoons (45 g/1.6 oz) ghee or other healthy cooking fat, divided
1 small (70 g/2.5 oz) yellow onion, chopped
3 cloves garlic, minced
1 cup (240 ml) bone broth (page 33) or beef stock
2 tablespoons (30 ml) rice wine or white wine vinegar
2 tablespoons (30 ml) coconut aminos
2 bay leaves
½ teaspoon coarse Korean red pepper
1.3 pounds (600 g) kimchi
Suggested side: cauli-rice (page 35)

GARNISH:

2 tablespoons (30 ml) toasted sesame oil
2 tablespoons (18 g/0.6 oz) sesame seeds
2 medium (30 g/1.1 oz) spring onions, sliced

Instructions

Preheat the slow cooker. Cut the beef into 1½-inch (4-cm) chunks, and season with salt and pepper. To brown the beef, grease a large heavy-based saucepan or Dutch oven with half of the ghee. Cook the beef in batches until browned on all sides and transfer to the slow cooker.

Grease the saucepan with the remaining ghee. Add the onion and cook over medium-high heat for 5 to 8 minutes, until lightly browned. Add the garlic and cook for a minute. Pour in the bone broth, rice wine, and coconut aminos. Bring to a boil, scraping the browned bits off the bottom. Pour into the slow cooker over the browned beef. Add the bay leaves, ½ teaspoon of black pepper, Korean red pepper, and kimchi. Stir to combine, cover with a lid, and cook for 4 hours on high or for 8 hours on low.

If serving with cauli-rice, ladle 1 to 2 cups (120 to 240 ml) of the cooking juices from the slow cooker into a saucepan with uncooked cauliflower rice, and cook for 5 to 8 minutes over medium heat.

To serve, drizzle with the sesame oil and sprinkle with the sesame seeds and spring onion. To store, let it cool, and refrigerate for up to 4 days or freeze for up to 3 months.

NUTRITION FACTS PER SERVING (WITHOUT SUGGESTED SIDE):
Total carbs: 6.9 g / Fiber: 2.7 g / Net carbs: 4.2 g / Protein: 32.1 g / Fat: 41.1 g / Energy: 540 kcal
Macronutrient ratio: Calories from carbs (3%), protein (25%), fat (72%)

{ Chapter 4 }

SAVORY ROASTS & CASSEROLES

Roasts and casseroles are really convenient because you can cook affordable meat cuts in bulk, freeze, and enjoy them later. All you have to do is prepare the ingredients, throw them in a slow cooker, and let it do its magic. To make defrosting and reheating easy, freeze the dishes in appropriate-sized containers or freezer bags.

This chapter features all-time favorites from all over the world. All of these dishes have something else in common: they require minimal prep time! You can now enjoy several European classics, Indian curries, African tagines, or American favorites. These recipes will help you cook crowd-pleasing dishes that are easy to prepare and packed with flavor. This means you can spend less time in the kitchen and more time with your family and friends.

MAKES: 8 servings
PREPARATION TIME: 25 minutes
COOKING TIME: 4 hours

Slow Cooker Eggplant Parmesan

Eggplant parm is usually off-menu on a low-carb lifestyle, because the eggplant slices are often doused in breadcrumbs. Not in this version, though! Whether you follow a vegetarian keto diet year-round or just don't feel like eating meat tonight, you can feel free to indulge in this filling, flavorful, keto-friendly casserole.

Ingredients

2 tablespoons (30 g/1.1 oz) ghee or other healthy cooking fat
3 medium (1 kg/2.2 lb) eggplants
Salt and ground black pepper
1 recipe marinara sauce (page 19)
2 cups (480 g/16.9 oz) full-fat ricotta cheese
2 cups (226 g/8 oz) shredded mozzarella cheese, divided
1 cup (90 g/3.2 oz) grated Parmesan cheese, divided
¼ cup (60 ml) extra-virgin olive oil
Fresh basil for garnish

Instructions

Preheat a 5- to 6-quart (4.7- to 5.7-L) slow cooker and grease it with the ghee. Using a sharp knife, slice the eggplant widthwise into thin ¼-inch (½-cm) slices. Season with salt on both sides and set aside for 20 minutes. Use a paper towel to pat dry any excess moisture.

In the meantime, mix the marinara sauce, ricotta cheese, mozzarella, and Parmesan (reserve some mozzarella and Parmesan for topping). Mix and season with salt and pepper to taste.

Place the first layer of the eggplant slices in the slow cooker. Top with half of the cheese mixture. Add another eggplant layer, a cheese layer, and finally the last eggplant layer. Top with the reserved cheese. Place 2 layers of high-absorbent paper towels or a tea towel on top of the ceramic bowl and cover with a lid. Cook on high for 4 hours or on low for 8 hours. To serve, drizzle with the olive oil and garnish with fresh basil leaves. To store, let it cool, and refrigerate for up to 5 days, freeze for up to 3 months.

NUTRITION FACTS PER SERVING:
Total carbs: 12.8 g / Fiber: 4.3 g / Net carbs: 8.5 g / Protein: 19.8 g / Fat: 33.2 g / Energy: 422 kcal
Macronutrient ratio: Calories from carbs (8%), protein (19%), fat (73%)

MAKES: 4 servings
PREPARATION TIME: 15 minutes
COOKING TIME: 2 to 3 hours

Fish Ball Tagine with Harissa

Packed with aromatics like garlic, cumin, and harissa, this Tunisian favorite is perfect with cauliflower rice to help soak up its rich sauce. These fish balls can be prepared in advance and frozen—then just add them to the freshly made sauce.

Ingredients

FISH BALLS:

- **1 small (70 g/2.5 oz) yellow onion, roughly chopped**
- **2 cloves garlic, sliced**
- **1 teaspoon ground cumin**
- **2 tablespoons (30 g/1.1 oz) mild Harissa Paste (page 27)**
- **½ teaspoon fine sea salt, or to taste**
- **Ground black pepper**
- **1.1 pounds (500 g) white fish (such as cod or haddock), skinless, boneless, and cut into chunks**
- **1 large egg**
- **¼ cup (30 g/1.1 oz) coconut flour**
- **1 tablespoon (4 g/0.2 oz) chopped cilantro**
- **1 tablespoon (4 g/0.2 oz) parsley**
- **¼ cup (55 g/1.9 oz) ghee or other healthy cooking fat**

Instructions

Preheat the slow cooker. Place all the aromatics for the fish balls in a food processor: onion, garlic, cumin, harissa paste, salt, and pepper to taste. Process until smooth, and add the fish. Pulse until well combined. Place the fish mixture in a bowl and combine with the egg, coconut flour, and fresh herbs. Using your hands, create 20 fish balls (each about 35 g/1.2 oz) and set aside.

To brown the fish balls, heat a large skillet greased with the ghee and cook the fish balls over medium-high heat for 2 minutes on each side, turning with a fork until browned on all sides and cooked through. (Don't turn too soon or they will crumble.) Transfer the fish balls to the slow cooker.

For the sacue, add the harissa, garlic, tomatoes, stock, and coconut butter to the pan where you browned the fish balls. Season with salt and pepper to taste. Bring to a boil and mix until the coconut butter is dissolved. Then pour into the slow cooker over the fish balls. Cover with a lid and cook on low for 2 to 3 hours.

When done, garnish with fresh herbs. Serve with plain or flavored cauliflower rice (page 35). To store, let it cool, and keep in an airtight container in the fridge for up to 4 days or freeze for up to 3 months.

NUTRITION FACTS PER SERVING (5 FISH BALLS):
Total carbs: 11.2 g / Fiber: 4.4 g / Net carbs: 6.8 g / Protein: 28.2 g / Fat: 24.2 g / Energy: 378 kcal
Macronutrient ratio: Calories from carbs (8%), protein (32%), fat (60%)

SAUCE:

1 tablespoon (15 g/0.5 oz) mild Harissa Paste (page 27)

1 clove garlic, minced

1 cup (240 g/8.5 oz) chopped canned tomatoes

1 cup (240 ml) chicken stock (page 22) or fish stock (page 23)

2 tablespoons (32 g/1.1 oz) coconut butter or almond butter

Salt and pepper

Freshly chopped parsley or cilantro for garnish

Suggested side: cauli-rice (page 35) or shirataki rice (page 15)

TIPS: Using a tagine dish? Preheat the oven to 350°F (175°C, or gas mark 4). Prepare the sauce with an additional ½ cup (120 ml) stock or water and pour into the tagine dish. Add the fish balls, cover with a lid, and bake for 20 to 25 minutes.

Using a skillet? Add ½ cup (120 ml) stock or water and cook the fish balls in the sauce over medium heat for 10 to 15 minutes.

MAKES: 8 servings
PREPARATION TIME: 20 minutes
COOKING TIME: 5 to 6 hours

Chicken Tikka Masala

There's nothing as comforting as tender chicken cooked in creamy coconut milk and a homemade curry paste, so put down that take-out menu and get ready to make the best—and easiest!—keto-friendly chicken tikka masala you've ever tasted.

Ingredients

- **¼ cup (55 g/1.9 oz) ghee or other healthy cooking fat**
- **1 small (70 g/2.5 oz) yellow onion, chopped**
- **1 recipe Tikka Masala Curry Paste (page 17)**
- **1 large (240 g/8.5 oz) tomato, diced (or use canned diced tomatoes)**
- **1½ cup (360 ml) chicken stock (page 22)**
- **2.7 pounds (1.2 kg) boneless and skinless chicken thighs, cut into 1½-inch (4-cm) chunks**
- **1½ cans (600 ml/20 fl oz) coconut milk**
- **Salt and pepper**
- **Suggested sides: cauli-rice (page 35) or shirataki rice (page 15)**
- **Optional: ⅓ cup (30 g/1.1 oz) flaked toasted almonds and fresh cilantro for garnish**

Instructions

Preheat the slow cooker. Grease a large heavy-based saucepan or Dutch oven with the ghee. Add the onion and cook over medium-high heat for 5 to 8 minutes, or until lightly browned. Add the tikka masala paste and cook for a minute, stirring frequently. Mix in the tomatoes and stock, and transfer the mixture to the slow cooker. Add the chicken chunks, cover with a lid, and cook on low for 4 to 6 hours. Stir in the coconut milk in the last 30 minutes of the cooking process.

When done, taste and season if needed. Serve with steamed cauli-rice or shirataki rice. Optionally, top with flaked toasted almonds and fresh cilantro. To store, let it cool, and refrigerate for up to 4 days or freeze for up to 3 months.

NUTRITION FACTS PER SERVING:
Total carbs: 8.5 g / Fiber: 2.6 g / Net carbs: 5.9 g / Protein: 32.7 g / Fat: 34.7 g / Energy: 468 kcal
Macronutrient ratio: Calories from carbs (5%), protein (28%), fat (67%)

MAKES: 8 servings
PREPARATION TIME: 20 minutes
COOKING TIME: 6 hours

Chicken Paprikash

This paprika-spiked Hungarian dish is really easy to prepare, and it's a major crowd-pleaser, too. Make a batch next time unexpected guests turn up, and ladle it over cauli-rice (page 35) or shirataki rice (page 15).

Ingredients

8 large (1.6 kg/3.5 lb) bone-in chicken thighs, trimmed of excess fat and skin (or 1.2 kg/2.7 lb boneless chicken)
Salt and pepper
2 tablespoons (30 g/1.1 oz) ghee or other healthy cooking fat, divided
1 medium (110 g/3.9 oz) yellow onion, chopped
2 cloves garlic, minced
1 medium (120 g/4.2 oz) red bell pepper, sliced
1 medium (120 g/4.2 oz) green bell pepper, sliced
1 cup (240 ml) chicken stock (page 22), divided
1 teaspoon dried marjoram
¼ cup (28 g/1 oz) paprika, divided
1 cup (240 g/8.5 oz) canned chopped tomatoes
4 egg yolks
1 cup (230 g/8.1 oz) full-fat sour cream
Fresh parsley for garnish
Suggested sides: cauli-rice (page 35) or shirataki rice (page 15)

Instructions

Preheat the slow cooker. Season the chicken thighs with salt on all sides. Heat a large skillet or casserole dish greased with 1 tablespoon (15 g) of the ghee. Once hot, add the chicken thighs in a single layer, skin-side down. Cook over medium-high heat for 5 minutes. Turn on the other side and cook for another 3 minutes. Remove the chicken from the pan and set aside on a plate.

Grease the pan with the remaining 1 tablespoon (15 g) ghee. Add the onion and cook over medium-high heat for 5 to 8 minutes, or until lightly browned. Add the garlic and peppers. Cook for a minute and add ½ cup (120 ml) of the chicken stock, marjoram, black pepper to taste, and 1 tablespoon (7 g) of the paprika. Add the tomatoes and heat through.

Transfer the mixture to a slow cooker and add back the browned chicken thighs. Cook on low for 5 hours. After 5 hours, use tongs to gently remove the chicken thighs and set aside on a plate. Beat the egg yolks with the remaining ½ cup (120 ml) chicken stock. Slowly drizzle into the slow cooker while stirring. Add the remaining 3 tablespoons (21 g) paprika and sour cream, and combine well. Add back the chicken, cover with a lid, and cook for another hour. When done, garnish with fresh parsley, taste, and season if needed. Serve with steamed cauli-rice or shirataki rice.

TIP: Are you dairy-free? Instead of 1 cup (230 g/8.1 oz) full-fat sour cream, try ¾ cup (180 g/6.4 oz) coconut cream with 2 tablespoons (30 ml) lemon juice or apple cider vinegar.

NUTRITION FACTS PER SERVING (WITHOUT SIDE DISH):
Total carbs: 7.2 g / Fiber: 2.3 g / Net carbs: 4.9 g / Protein: 24.8 g / Fat: 56 g / Energy: 632 kcal
Macronutrient ratio: Calories from carbs (3%), protein (16%), fat (81%)

MAKES: 4 servings
PREPARATION TIME: 20 minutes
COOKING TIME: 6 hours

Whole Slow Cooker Chicken

Believe it or not, it's super-easy to roast a whole chicken in a slow cooker. The skin won't get crispy, as with oven roasting, but the meat becomes amazingly tender and juicy. For best results, lather the chicken in fragrant herb-and-spice rubs before cooking.

Ingredients

CHICKEN:

1 whole chicken (about 1.4 kg/3 lb, bones included), will yield about 50% meat
1 tablespoon (15 g/0.5 oz) ghee or other healthy cooking fat, divided
1 small (70 g/2.5 oz) yellow onion, chopped
2 cloves garlic, minced

CURRIED RUB:

2 tablespoons (30 g/1.1 oz) ghee or other healthy cooking fat, softened
2 teaspoons curry powder
1 teaspoon fine sea salt, or to taste
½ teaspoon onion powder
½ teaspoon garlic powder
½ teaspoon ground black pepper
½ teaspoon paprika
¼ teaspoon ground ginger
¼ teaspoon ground caraway

Instructions

Preheat the slow cooker. Rinse the chicken under cold water, then pat dry inside and out using a paper towel. Place on a chopping board.

In a bowl, combine all the ingredients for the rub and set aside.

Grease a large heavy-based saucepan or Dutch oven with the ghee. Add the onion and cook over medium-high heat for 5 to 8 minutes, until lightly browned. Add the garlic, cook for 1 minute, and transfer to the slow cooker.

Use your hands to create a pocket between the breasts, thighs, and drumsticks and the chicken skin. Push half of the flavored rub under the skin and rub the remaining mixture all over the chicken. Tuck the wing tips under the chicken and tie the legs together using kitchen string.

Grease the saucepan where you cooked the onion with the remaining tablespoon (15 g) of ghee and cook the chicken until browned all over. Transfer to the slow cooker on top of the browned onion and garlic. Cook on low for 6 hours. Serve with low-carb veggies or Make-Ahead Slow Cooker Mash (page 32). To store, let it cool, and refrigerate for up to 3 days.

NUTRITION FACTS PER SERVING (¼ CHICKEN):
Total carbs: 3.5 g / Fiber: 1 g / Net carbs: 2.5 g / Protein: 33.1 g / Fat: 42.5 g / Energy: 529 kcal
Macronutrient ratio: Calories from carbs (2%), protein (25%), fat (73%)

MAKES: 4 servings (20 meatballs)
PREPARATION TIME: 15 minutes
COOKING TIME: 3 to 4 hours

Festive Turkey Meatballs

We all know that homemade cranberry sauce goes best with roast turkey, especially during the festive season. Here, though, I've transformed that classic pairing into tender, juicy turkey meatballs drenched in a tangy cranberry "gravy." Your guests will be seriously impressed!

Ingredients

MEATBALLS:

- **¼ cup (55 g/1.9 oz) ghee or other healthy cooking fat, divided**
- **1 small (70 g/2.5 oz) yellow onion, chopped**
- **2 cloves garlic, minced**
- **1.1 pounds (500 g) ground turkey**
- **1 large egg**
- **2 tablespoons (16 g/0.6 oz) coconut flour or ½ cup (50 g/1.8 oz) almond flour**
- **½ teaspoon dried thyme**
- **2 tablespoons (8 g/0.3 oz) freshly chopped parsley, plus more for garnish**
- **½ teaspoon fine sea salt, or to taste**
- **¼ teaspoon ground black pepper**

SAUCE:

- **½ cup (125 g/4.4 oz) Cranberry Sauce (page 29)**
- **½ cup (120 ml) chicken stock (page 22)**
- **Suggested side dish: Make-Ahead Slow Cooker Mash (page 32)**

Instructions

Preheat the slow cooker. Grease a large skillet with 2 tablespoons (30 g) of the ghee. Add the onion and cook over medium-high heat for 5 to 8 minutes, until lightly browned. Add the garlic, cook for another minute, and set aside.

Place the turkey, egg, coconut flour, thyme, fresh parsley, salt, pepper, and cooked onions with garlic in a bowl. Mix until well combined. Using your hands, create 20 meatballs (about 32 g/1.1 oz each).

To brown the meatballs, grease a large pan with the remaining 2 tablespoons (30 g) ghee and place over medium heat. When hot, add the meatballs in a single layer. Cook for 2 minutes on each side, turning with a fork until browned on all sides and cooked through. Transfer the meatballs to the slow cooker.

Add the cranberry sauce and chicken stock to the skillet where you cooked the meatballs and bring to a boil. Cook for a minute, and pour into the slow cooker over the meatballs. Cook on low for 3 to 4 hours. Serve with Make-Ahead Slow Cooker Mash (page 32) or low-carb veggies. To store, let it cool, and refrigerate for up to 4 days.

NUTRITION FACTS PER SERVING (5 MEATBALLS):
Total carbs: 6.7 g / Fiber: 2.2 g / Net carbs: 4.5 g / Protein: 24.4 g / Fat: 31.9 g / Energy: 413 kcal
Macronutrient ratio: Calories from carbs (5%), protein (24%), fat (71%)

MAKES: 6 servings
PREPARATION TIME: 20 minutes
COOKING TIME: 4 to 5 hours

Beef Bourguignon

This classic French dish might sound intimidating, but it's actually incredibly easy to make. Dry red wine lends an earthy, rich flavor to the slow-cooked meat, which is wonderful with roasted green beans or steamed leafy greens. (Only add the carrot if it fits within your daily carbohydrate limit.)

Ingredients

BOUQUET GARNI:

2 sprigs fresh parsley and thyme
1 teaspoon peppercorns
3 whole cloves
3 bay leaves

STEW:

2 pounds (900 g) beef chuck steak or brisket
Salt
3 tablespoons (45 g/1.6 oz) ghee or other healthy cooking fat, divided
1 medium (110 g/3.9 oz) white onion, chopped
3 cloves garlic, crushed
Optional: 1 medium (60 g/2.1 oz) carrot, sliced
1 bottle (750 ml) dry red wine such as Burgundy
1 tablespoon (15 g/0.5 oz) unsweetened tomato paste
8 slices (240 g/8.5 oz) bacon
4 cups (300 g/10.6 oz) sliced white mushrooms
1 teaspoon fine sea salt, or to taste
Suggested side: Make-Ahead Slow Cooker Mash (page 32) or roasted green beans

Instructions

Preheat the slow cooker. Make the bouquet garni by placing all the herbs in a piece of cheesecloth and tying with unwaxed kitchen string.

Cut the beef into large chunks and season with some salt. Heat a Dutch oven or a heavy-based pot greased with 2 tablespoons (30 g/1.1 oz) of the ghee. Fry the beef chunks in batches over medium-high heat until golden brown on all sides, about 5 minutes. Remove the chunks from the pot and place them in the slow cooker.

Add the onion, crushed garlic, and carrot (if using) to the pot where you browned the beef and lower the heat. Pour in the red wine and add the tomato paste. Bring to a boil and mix well with a spatula, scraping the caramelized cooking juices from the bottom of the pot. Pour into the slow cooker. Add the bouquet garni, cover with a lid, and cook on high for 4 to 5 hours. Remove the bouquet garni when the meat is cooked.

Grease a pan with the remaining 1 tablespoon (15 g) ghee and crisp up the bacon over medium heat for about 5 minutes. Add the mushrooms and cook for another 4 to 5 minutes, or until tender and browned. Take off the heat and place in the slow cooker with the beef. Mix until well combined. Serve with Make-Ahead Slow Cooker Mash (page 32) or roasted green beans. To store, let it cool, and refrigerate for up to 4 days or freeze for up to 3 months.

NUTRITION FACTS PER SERVING:
Total carbs: 8.3 g / Fiber: 1.4 g / Net carbs: 6.9 g / Protein: 36.7 g / Fat: 45 g / Energy: 678 kcal
Macronutrient ratio: Calories from carbs (5%), protein (25%), fat (70%)

MAKES: 8 servings
PREPARATION TIME: 20 minutes
COOKING TIME: 4 to 5 hours

Osso Buco with Gremolata

Osso buco, which translates as "pierced bone" in Italian, involves cooking veal shanks on low for several hours, and they're well worth the wait: they're amazingly tender and juicy, thanks, in part, to the luscious bone marrow. Serve with a spoonful of garlicky, lemony gremolata.

Ingredients

BOUQUET GARNI:

3 sprigs fresh thyme
1 sprig fresh rosemary
2 bay leaves
2 cloves
1 teaspoon whole black peppercorns

STEW:

4 whole bone-in veal shanks (1.8 kg/4 lb), will yield about 60% meat
Salt and pepper
3 tablespoons (45 g/1.6 oz) ghee or other healthy cooking fat, divided
1 small (70 g/2.5 oz) yellow onion, sliced
2 cloves garlic, minced
3 large (192 g/6.8 oz) celery stalks, sliced
1 cup (240 ml) bone broth (page 33) or water
1 cup (240 g/8.5 oz) canned or fresh diced tomatoes
2 tablespoons (30 g/1.1 oz) unsweetened tomato paste
1 cup (240 ml) dry white wine

Suggested sides: cauli-rice (page 35), Make-Ahead Slow Cooker Mash (page 32) or other low-carb vegetable sides

GREMOLATA:

½ cup (30 g/1.1 oz) chopped parsley
2 cloves garlic, crushed
Zest from 1 lemon

Instructions

Preheat the slow cooker. Make the bouquet garni by placing all the herbs in a piece of cheesecloth and tying with unwaxed kitchen string.

Pat dry the veal shanks using a paper towel. Secure the shanks to the bone with kitchen string, and season with salt and pepper.

Grease a large heavy-based saucepan or Dutch oven with half of the ghee. Brown the veal shanks on all sides over high heat. Remove the shanks and set aside.

Grease the saucepan with the remaining ghee. Add the onion and cook over medium-high heat for 5 to 8 minutes, or until lightly browned. Add the garlic, celery, bone broth, tomatoes, tomato paste, and white wine. Transfer to the slow cooker and add the prepared bouquet garni. Add the browned veal shanks in a single layer, and cover with a lid. Cook on high for 4 hours or on low for 8 hours. When done, remove and discard the bouquet garni and kitchen string. Serve with cauli-rice or other low-carb veggies. To store, refrigerate for up to 4 days, or shred the meat off the bones and freeze for up to 3 months.

NUTRITION FACTS PER SERVING:
Total carbs: 4.5 g / Fiber: 1.1 g / Net carbs: 3.4 g / Protein: 24.5 g / Fat: 23 g / Energy: 350 kcal
Macronutrient ratio: Calories from carbs (4%), protein (31%), fat (65%)

MAKES: 4 servings
PREPARATION TIME: 25 minutes
COOKING TIME: 6 hours

Stuffed Cabbage Rolls with Spicy Hollandaise

Once they've been blanched, vitamin-C-rich cabbage leaves are handy vehicles for all sorts of fillings, like these fun-to-eat low-carb cabbage rolls, which are packed with beef, Cauli-Rice, and spices.

Ingredients

CABBAGE ROLLS:

1.1 pounds (500 g) minced beef
2 cups (240 g/8.5 oz) uncooked cauli-rice (page 35)
1 small (70 g/2.5 oz) yellow onion, chopped
2 cloves garlic, minced
1 large egg
½ teaspoon fine sea salt
¼ teaspoon ground black pepper
1 teaspoon Dijon mustard
2 tablespoons (8 g/0.3 oz) freshly chopped parsley
1 teaspoon paprika
1 medium or 2 small (500 g/1.1 lb) savoy cabbage
1 cup (240 ml) bone broth (page 33)

Instructions

Preheat the slow cooker. In a bowl, combine the the beef, cauli-rice, onion, garlic, egg, salt, pepper, Dijon mustard, parsley, and paprika.

Separate the outer 12 cabbage leaves and place them in a pot of boiling salted water. Blanch until limp, 1 to 2 minutes. Transfer the leaves to a large bowl filled with ice water. Drain and pat dry. Remove the core of the cabbage, slice the remaining leaves, place them in the slow cooker, and add the bone broth.

Place the cabbage leaves on a chopping board. Using a paring knife, shave down the thick cabbage stems in the middle. Do not cut through the cabbage leaves. Place some of the meat filling (about 70 g/2.5 oz per leaf) in the middle of the cabbage. (The exact amount depends on the size of the leaf. Do not overfill the leaves.) Roll the cabbage leaf up, folding both sides over the filling, creating a small parcel. Place the cabbage parcels seam-side down in the slow cooker in two or three layers, and cook on low for 6 hours.

To make the hollandaise sauce, gently melt the butter and set aside. Fill a medium saucepan with 1 cup (240 ml) water and bring to a boil. In a separate bowl, mix the egg yolks with the lemon juice, water, and Dijon mustard. (Use the leftover egg whites to make Sourdough Keto Buns on page 34).

Place the bowl over the saucepan filled with water. (The water should not touch the bottom of the bowl.) Keep mixing until the sauce starts to thicken. Slowly pour the melted butter into the

NUTRITION FACTS PER SERVING (3 CABBAGE ROLLS WITH 3 TABLESPOONS [40 G/1.4 OZ] OF HOLLANDAISE):
Total carbs: 14.1 g / Fiber: 5.7 g / Net carbs: 8.4 g / Protein: 30.3 g / Fat: 49.4 g / Energy: 613 kcal
Macronutrient ratio: Calories from carbs (6%), protein (20%), fat (74%)

SPICY HOLLANDAISE:

6 tablespoons (85 g/3 oz) butter, ghee, or bacon grease

3 egg yolks

3 tablespoons (45 ml) lemon juice

2 to 3 tablespoons (30 to 45 ml) water

¾ teaspoon Dijon mustard

1 tablespoon (15 g/0.5 oz) sriracha sauce or tomato paste for non-spicy

mixture until thick and creamy, and stir constantly. If the sauce is too thick, add a splash of water. Mix in the sriracha sauce and set aside. Cover with a lid and keep warm for up to 2 hours. Serve with the cooked stuffed cabbage leaves. Do not reheat the hollandaise or it will separate. Always make a fresh batch. To store the cabbage rolls, let them cool, and refrigerate for up to 4 days or freeze for up to 3 months.

MAKES: 6 servings
PREPARATION TIME: 20 minutes
COOKING TIME: 4 to 5 hours + marinating

Beef Short Ribs with Coleslaw

What's the best way to make perfectly tender beef ribs? Pop them into a slow cooker, of course: afterward, it takes just a few minutes to finish them off in the oven. And for a complete meal, you'll want to serve them alongside crisp, creamy, tangy coleslaw.

Ingredients

SPICE RUB:

1 tablespoon (10 g/0.3 oz) garlic powder
1 tablespoon (7 g/0.2 oz) onion powder
2 teaspoons (5 g/0.2 oz) paprika
2 teaspoons fine sea salt
1 tablespoon (5 g/0.2 oz) oregano
¼ teaspoon cayenne pepper

SHORT RIBS:

4 pounds (1.8 kg) beef short ribs, will yield about 50% meat
½ cup (120 g/4.2 oz) Sweet & Sour BBQ Sauce (page 28), plus optionally more to serve with

COLESLAW:

1.3 pounds (600 g) sliced green or white cabbage, core removed
1 small (60 g/2.1 oz) red onion, sliced
½ cup (110 g/3.9 oz) mayonnaise (page 19)
3 tablespoons (45 ml) fresh lemon juice
¼ cup (15 g/0.5 oz) chopped parsley or chives
½ teaspoon celery seeds
Salt and pepper

Instructions

Preheat the slow cooker and pour in ¼ cup (60 ml) of water. Prepare the rub by mixing all the spices and set aside.

Pat dry the ribs using a paper towel and cover the short ribs in the spice rub, pressing it all over the ribs. Optionally, cover and marinate in the fridge for up to 8 hours. Transfer the ribs to the slow cooker and cook on high for 4 to 5 hours, until the meat is tender.

Prepare the coleslaw. Using your food processor's slicing blade, thinly slice the cabbage, and then place in a large mixing bowl. Add the red onion, mayonnaise, lemon juice, parsley, and celery seeds. Season with salt and pepper to taste, and mix well.

After 4 to 5 hours of cooking the ribs, using tongs, remove the ribs from the slow cooker and place on a baking sheet lined with heavy-duty parchment paper. Preheat the broiler. Brush the ribs with the BBQ sauce on all sides and place the ribs under the broiler. Cook on high for 8 to 10 minutes, turning halfway through. Serve with the prepared coleslaw. To store both the ribs and the coleslaw, refrigerate for up to 4 days. To freeze the ribs, shred off the bones and freeze for up to 3 months (meat only).

NUTRITION FACTS PER SERVING:
Total carbs: 11.7 g / Fiber: 4.1 g / Net carbs: 7.6 g / Protein: 28.5 g / Fat: 44.4 g / Energy: 547 kcal
Macronutrient ratio: Calories from carbs (6%), protein (21%), fat (73%)

MAKES: 8 servings
PREPARATION TIME: 15 minutes
COOKING TIME: 4 to 5 hours

Slow Cooker Beef Fajitas

Made with low-carb Keto Tortillas (page 30), these beef fajitas are the real deal. Create a dinnertime "fajita bar" by offering toppings—like sour cream, diced avocado, tomatoes, green pepper, grated Cheddar or Manchego cheese, lime wedges, and cilantro—separately, and let everyone build their own. That's half the fun!

Ingredients

2.65 pounds (1.2 kg) beef chuck steak
1 teaspoon salt, or to taste
Ground black pepper
2 tablespoons (30 g/1.1 oz) ghee or other healthy cooking fat, divided
1 small (70 g/2.5 oz) yellow onion, sliced
3 cloves garlic, minced
14.1 ounces (400 g) canned chopped tomatoes
2 tablespoons (30 g/1.1 oz) unsweetened tomato paste
2 teaspoons ground cumin
2 teaspoons ground coriander
1 teaspoon smoked paprika
1 teaspoon chili powder
8 Keto Tortillas of choice, soft or crisped up into taco shells (see page 30)
Suggested sides: sour cream, diced avocado, tomatoes, green pepper, grated Cheddar or Manchego cheese, lime wedges, and cilantro

Instructions

Preheat the slow cooker. Cut the beef into large (about 1½-inch/4-cm) chunks and season with salt and pepper. To brown the beef, grease a large heavy-based saucepan or Dutch oven with half of the ghee. Cook the beef in batches until browned on all sides and transfer to the slow cooker.

Grease the saucepan with the remaining ghee. Add the onion and cook over medium-high heat for 5 to 8 minutes, until lightly browned. Add the garlic and cook for a minute. Add the tomatoes and bring to a boil, scraping the browned bits from the bottom of the pan. Pour into the slow cooker over the browned beef. Add the tomato paste, cumin, coriander, paprika, and chili powder. Cover with a lid. Cook on high for 3 to 4 hours or on low for 6 to 8 hours.

When done, shred the beef with a fork. Serve with the tortillas and sides of choice. To store, refrigerate the meat for up to 5 days or freeze for up to 3 months.

NUTRITION FACTS PER SERVING (MEAT + CURRIED TORTILLA):
Total carbs: 12 g / Fiber: 7.1 g / Net carbs: 4.9 g / Protein: 34.8 g / Fat: 41.3 g / Energy: 554 kcal
Macronutrient ratio: Calories from carbs (4%), protein (26%), fat (70%)

MAKES: 6 servings
PREPARATION TIME: 15 minutes
COOKING TIME: 8 hours

Greek Stifado

One thing's for sure: Greeks know their way around the kitchen. This popular dish is proof: It's served in almost every Greek tavern, and it features beef cooked in a rich tomato-and red-wine sauce that's enhanced by fragrant oregano and warming spices, like cloves, nutmeg, and allspice.

Ingredients

2 pounds (900 g) beef chuck
¾ teaspoon fine sea salt, or to taste
Ground black pepper
¼ cup (55 g/1.9 oz) ghee or other healthy cooking fat, divided
1 small (70 g/2.5 oz) yellow onion, chopped
2 cloves garlic, minced
1½ cups (360 ml) dry red wine
¼ cup (60 ml) red wine vinegar
1 cup (240 g/8.5) canned chopped tomatoes
1 tablespoon (15 g/0.5 oz) unsweetened tomato paste
2 bay leaves
2 teaspoons dried oregano
¼ teaspoon ground cinnamon
¼ teaspoon ground allspice
¼ teaspoon ground cloves
⅛ teaspoon ground nutmeg
1.3 pounds (600 g) baby turnips, halved, or regular turnips, diced
Fresh herbs for garnish (basil, oregano, or parsley)

Instructions

Preheat the slow cooker. Cut the beef into large (about 1½-inch/4-cm) chunks and season with salt and pepper. To brown the beef, grease a large heavy-based saucepan or Dutch oven with half of the ghee. Cook the beef in batches until browned on all sides and transfer to the slow cooker.

Grease the saucepan with the remaining ghee. Add the onion and cook over medium-high heat for 5 to 8 minutes, until lightly browned. Add the garlic and cook for a minute. Add the red wine, wine vinegar, tomatoes, tomato paste, bay leaves, oregano, cinnamon, allspice, cloves, and nutmeg. Bring to a boil, scraping the browned bits off the bottom. Pour into the slow cooker over the beef, cover with a lid, and cook on low for 8 hours.

Add the turnips in the last 2 to 3 hours of the cooking process, and stir to combine with the meat and juices. When done, remove the bay leaves, garnish with fresh herbs, and serve. To store, let it cool, and refrigerate for up to 4 days or freeze for up to 3 months.

NUTRITION FACTS PER SERVING:
Total carbs: 11.8 g / Fiber: 2.9 g / Net carbs: 8.9 g / Protein: 30.4 g / Fat: 36.4 g / Energy: 543 kcal
Macronutrient ratio: Calories from carbs (7%), protein (25%), fat (68%)

MAKES: 8 servings
PREPARATION TIME: 20 minutes
COOKING TIME: 4 to 5 hours + marinating

BBQ Pulled Pork Sliders

Rich, tender, juicy pulled pork is at its best when paired with a punchy side dish like spicy, homemade coleslaw. Add a couple of Sourdough Keto Buns (page 34), and you've got genuine low-carb soul food.

Ingredients

SPICE RUB:

1 tablespoon ground cumin
1 teaspoon garlic powder
1 teaspoon onion powder
1 teaspoon paprika
1 teaspoon chili powder
1 teaspoon mustard powder
½ teaspoon ground black pepper
1½ teaspoons fine sea salt

PORK SLIDERS:

3.3 pounds (1.5 kg) bone-in pork shoulder or 2.65 pounds (1.2 kg) boneless pork shoulder
¼ cup (60 ml) water
¾ cup (180 g/6.4 oz) Sweet & Sour BBQ sauce (page 28)
Suggestions (per serving): 1 or 2 mini Sourdough Keto Buns (page 34)

SPICY SLAW:

1 pound (450 g) green cabbage, shredded
1 small (60 g/2.1 oz) red onion, sliced
1 piece (14 g/0.5 oz) jalapeño pepper, chopped
⅓ cup (73/2.6 oz) mayonnaise (page 19)
3 tablespoons (45 ml) fresh lime juice
1 teaspoon Dijon mustard
¼ teaspoon red pepper flakes
2 tablespoons (8 g/0.3 oz) freshly chopped cilantro or parsley
Salt and pepper

Instructions

Preheat the slow cooker. Prepare the rub by mixing all the spices. Pat dry the pork using a paper towel and cover in the spice rub, pressing it all over and cover in plastic wrap, refrigerate, and let it marinate for 8 hours or up to 24 hours. (If you're short on time, marinating can be skipped.) Transfer to the slow cooker, add the water, and cook on high for 4 to 5 hours, until the meat is tender.

Prepare the spicy slaw by mixing all the ingredients: cabbage, red onion, jalapeño pepper, mayonnaise, lime juice, Dijon mustard, pepper flakes, cilantro, and salt and pepper to taste. Cover and refrigerate to let the flavors combine.

When the meat is cooked, shred it with two forks. Add the BBQ sauce and combine with the cooking juices. Serve the pork with the prepared slaw, and optionally with the buns. Keep leftovers refrigerated for up to 4 days, or freeze for up to 3 months.

NUTRITION FACTS PER SERVING (WITHOUT KETO BUNS):
Total carbs: 7.3 g / Fiber: 2.5 g / Net carbs: 4.8 g / Protein: 27.3 g / Fat: 36.6 g / Energy: 468 kcal
Macronutrient ratio: Calories from carbs (4%), protein (24%), fat (72%)

MAKES: 8 servings
PREPARATION TIME: 25 minutes
COOKING TIME: 8 hours

Moussaka

Laced with a simple, homemade béchamel sauce, this slow-cooker moussaka is the very best low-carb version of everyone's favorite Greek casserole.

Ingredients

MOUSSAKA:

- **2 medium (680 kg/1.5 lb) eggplants**
- **1 medium (400 g/14.1 oz) rutabaga, peeled**
- **1½ teaspoons fine sea salt, or to taste**
- **2 tablespoons (30 g/1.1 oz) ghee or other healthy cooking fat**
- **1 small (70 g/2.5 oz) yellow onion, chopped**
- **2 cloves garlic, minced**
- **2.2 pounds (1 kg) ground lamb**
- **3 tablespoons (12 g/0.4 oz) freshly chopped oregano or 1 tablespoon dried oregano**
- **3 tablespoons (12 g/0.4 oz) freshly chopped mint or 1 tablespoon dried mint**
- **1 teaspoon ground cinnamon**
- **½ teaspoon ground cloves**
- **1 bay leaf, crumbled**
- **¼ teaspoon ground black pepper**
- **2 tablespoons (30 g/1.1 oz) unsweetened tomato paste**
- **1 cup (240 ml) dry red wine**

Instructions

Preheat the slow cooker and grease with a small amount of ghee. Cut the eggplant and rutabaga into about ¼-inch (½-cm) slices. Season the eggplant and rutabaga slices with salt, and set aside for 20 minutes. Pat dry any excess moisture off the eggplant using a paper towel.

Meanwhile, grease a large heavy-based saucepan or Dutch oven with the ghee. Add the onion and cook over medium-high heat for 5 to 8 minutes, until lightly browned. Add the garlic and cook for a minute. Add the lamb and cook over medium heat until browned on all sides, about 5 minutes, stirring frequently. Add the oregano, mint, cinnamon, cloves, bay leaf, black pepper, tomato paste, and red wine. Cook for 5 to 8 minutes, or until the sauce is reduced by half. Season to taste and set aside.

To assemble the moussaka, place a layer of the rutabaga slices on the bottom of the slow cooker. Add a layer of eggplant slices (about a third of the amount), and half of the meat mixture. Add another third of rutabaga-eggplant slices and the remaining meat mixture. Top with the remaining rutabaga-eggplant slices. Cover with a lid and cook on low for 8 hours.

In the meantime, prepare the béchamel sauce. In a saucepan, mix the cream, egg yolks, nutmeg, and crumbled bay leaf. Cook over medium-low heat, stirring constantly, until it starts to thicken. Take off the heat and mix in 1 cup (90 g/3.2 oz) of the grated Parmesan cheese. After 6 hours of cooking the moussaka, pour in the béchamel sauce. Sprinkle with the remaining ½ cup (45 g) Parmesan cheese, cover with a lid, and cook for another

NUTRITION FACTS PER SERVING:
Total carbs: 14.7 g / Fiber: 4.7 g / Net carbs: 10 g / Protein: 31.4 g / Fat: 52.8 g / Energy: 685 kcal
Macronutrient ratio: Calories from carbs (6%), protein (20%), fat (74%)

BÉCHAMEL SAUCE:

1½ cups (360 ml) heavy whipping cream
4 egg yolks
¼ teaspoon ground nutmeg
1 bay leaf, crumbled
1½ cups (135 g/4.8 oz) grated Parmesan cheese, divided
Salt and pepper

2 hours. Optionally, you can crisp the moussaka in the oven at 400°F (200°C, or gas mark 6) for 5 to 8 minutes, or until the top is golden brown. Serve immediately, or let it cool and refrigerate for up to 4 days or freeze for up to 3 months.

MAKES: 6 servings
PREPARATION TIME: 20 minutes
COOKING TIME: 4 to 5 hours + marinating

BBQ Pork Ribs

Slow-cooking these pork ribs ensures that they're extra-tender; drenching them in a sugar-free mole barbeque sauce and roasting them in the oven afterwards adds dark, bewitching flavor. The result? A melt-in-the-mouth wonder.

Ingredients

MARINATED RIBS:

- **2 tablespoons (14 g/0.5 oz) smoked paprika or ancho chile powder**
- **1 tablespoon (9 g/0.3 oz) mustard powder**
- **2 teaspoons ground cumin**
- **1 teaspoon celery seeds**
- **1 teaspoon garlic powder**
- **1 teaspoon ground black pepper**
- **2 teaspoons fine sea salt**
- **¼ cup (40 g/1.4 oz) brown sugar substitute such as Sukrin, erythritol, or Swerve**
- **4 pounds (1.8 kg) pork spare ribs, will yield about 50% meat**
- **Suggested side: coleslaw (page 63)**

BBQ SAUCE:

- **Use ½ cup (120 g/4.2 oz) Sweet & Sour BBQ Sauce (page 28), or try the following variation by mixing these ingredients:**
- **¼ cup (60 g/2.1 oz) Sweet & Sour BBQ Sauce (page 28)**
- **1 heaping tablespoon (30 g/1.1 oz) Cranberry Sauce (page 29)**
- **1 tablespoon (15 ml) coconut or apple cider vinegar**
- **1 tablespoon (15 ml) coconut aminos**
- **1 tablespoons (5 g/0.2 oz) cocoa powder**

Instructions

Preheat the slow cooker and pour in ¼ cup (60 ml) of water. Prepare the rub by mixing all the spices and set aside. Pat dry the ribs using a paper towel and cover them in the spice rub, pressing it all over the ribs. Place the ribs in plastic wrap, refrigerate, and let them marinate for 8 hours or up to 24 hours. (If you're short on time, marinating can be skipped.) Transfer them to the slow cooker and cook on high for 4 to 5 hours, until the meat is tender.

When done, use tongs to carefully remove the ribs from the slow cooker and place them on a baking sheet lined with heavy-duty parchment paper. Preheat the broiler. Brush the BBQ sauce on both sides of the pork ribs and place under the broiler. Cook for 8 to 10 minutes, turning halfway through. Serve the ribs with coleslaw (page 63) or other low-carb veggie sides.

NUTRITION FACTS PER SERVING (WITHOUT SUGGESTED SIDE):
Total carbs: 4.8 g / Fiber: 1.9 g / Net carbs: 2.9 g / Protein: 24.5 g / Fat: 37 g / Energy: 451 kcal
Macronutrient ratio: Calories from carbs (3%), protein (22%), fat (75%)

MAKES: 8 servings
PREPARATION TIME: 15 minutes
COOKING TIME: 8 hours

Lamb Rogan Josh

This delectable, mildly spicy curry is a staple of Kashmiri cuisine. It's made with sweet tomatoes, warming chiles, and stimulating, aromatic spices like cardamom and cinnamon. If you like yours on the spicy side, add some chili powder for extra heat.

Ingredients

- **2.65 pounds (1.2 kg) boneless leg of lamb**
- **Salt and pepper**
- **¼ cup (55 g/1.9 oz) ghee or other healthy cooking fat, divided**
- **1 medium (110 g/3.9 oz) yellow onion, chopped**
- **1 recipe Rogan Josh Curry Paste (page 17)**
- **2 large (400 g/7.1 oz) tomatoes, diced (or use canned diced tomatoes)**
- **1 cup (240 ml) bone broth (page 33) or vegetable stock (page 22)**
- **2 bay leaves**
- **1 cup (230 g/8.1 oz) full-fat sour cream or creamed coconut milk (see page 21)**
- **Optional: ⅔ cup (60 g/2.1 oz) toasted flaked almonds and fresh cilantro for topping**
- **Suggested side: cauli-rice (page 35) or shirataki rice (page 15)**

Instructions

Preheat the slow cooker. Cut the lamb into 1½-inch (4-cm) chunks, and season with salt and pepper. Grease a large heavy-based saucepan or Dutch oven with half of the ghee. Cook the lamb in batches until browned on all sides and transfer to the slow cooker.

Grease the pan where you cooked the lamb with the remaining ghee. Add the onion and cook over medium-high heat for 5 to 8 minutes, until lightly browned. Add the Rogan Josh curry paste and cook for a minute, stirring frequently. Mix in the tomatoes, bone broth, and bay leaves, and transfer to the slow cooker. Cover with a lid. Cook on low for 8 hours or on high for 4 hours.

When done, discard the bay leaves and mix in the sour cream. Taste and season if needed. Optionally, top with toasted flaked almonds and fresh cilantro, and serve with steamed cauli-rice or shirataki rice. To store, let it cool, and refrigerate for up to 4 days or freeze for up to 3 months.

NUTRITION FACTS PER SERVING:
Total carbs: 7.6 g / Fiber: 2 g / Net carbs: 5.6 g / Protein: 29.7 g / Fat: 36.3 g / Energy: 477 kcal
Macronutrient ratio: Calories from carbs (5%), protein (25%), fat (70%)

MAKES: 8 servings
PREPARATION TIME: 15 minutes
COOKING TIME: 8 hours

Moroccan Lamb

Got a jar of homemade harissa paste (page 27) lingering in the fridge? Crack it open and put it to good use by making a batch of this North African classic, which features spiced lamb, rich broth, and plenty of green olives.

Ingredients

- **2.65 pounds (1.2 kg) boneless leg of lamb**
- **1 teaspoon fine sea salt, or to taste**
- **Ground black pepper**
- **3 tablespoons (45 g/1.6 oz) ghee or other healthy cooking fat, divided**
- **1 small (70 g/2.5 oz) yellow onion, chopped**
- **2 cloves garlic, minced**
- **3 large (192 g/6.8 oz) celery stalks, sliced**
- **2 medium (400 g/7.1 oz) tomatoes, diced (or use canned diced tomatoes)**
- **2 cups (480 ml) bone broth (page 33)**
- **¼ cup (63 g/2.2 oz) coconut butter or almond butter**
- **1 tablespoon (7 g/0.2 oz) paprika**
- **1 tablespoon (7 g/0.2 oz) onion powder**
- **1 teaspoon garlic powder**
- **3 tablespoons (45 g/1.6 oz) harissa paste (page 27)**
- **1 cup (100 g/3.5 oz) pitted green olives**
- **Suggested side: cauli-rice (page 35) or shirataki rice (page 15)**
- **Fresh cilantro or parsley for garnish**

Instructions

Preheat the slow cooker. Cut the lamb into 1½-inch (4-cm) chunks, and season with salt and pepper. To brown the lamb, grease a large heavy-based saucepan or Dutch oven with half of the ghee. Cook the lamb in batches until browned on all sides and transfer to the slow cooker.

Grease the pan where you cooked the lamb with the remaining ghee. Add the onion and cook over medium-high heat for 5 to 8 minutes, until lightly browned. Add the garlic, celery, tomatoes, bone broth, and coconut butter, and bring to a boil. Pour into the slow cooker. Add the paprika, onion powder, garlic powder, and harissa paste. Cover with a lid. Cook on low for 8 hours or on high for 4 hours. Stir in the olives in the last 30 to 60 minutes of the cooking process.

When done, taste and season if needed. Serve with steamed cauli-rice or shirataki rice. Garnish with fresh cilantro. To store, let it cool, and refrigerate for up to 4 days or freeze for up to 3 months.

NUTRITION FACTS PER SERVING (WITHOUT SUGGESTED SIDE):
Total carbs: 8.5 g / Fiber: 3.5 g / Net carbs: 5 g / Protein: 30.1 g / Fat: 34.4 g / Energy: 480 kcal
Macronutrient ratio: Calories from carbs (4%), protein (26%), fat (70%)

MAKES: 4 servings
PREPARATION TIME: 15 minutes
COOKING TIME: 8 hours

Irish Lamb Shanks

Traditional Irish stew is a simple yet delicious dish, but you can take it to the next level by using a couple of tricks: browning the meat before slow-cooking enhances the flavors, while adding the vegetables at the end of the cooking process makes them perfectly tender, but not mushy.

Ingredients

BOUQUET GARNI:

2 to 3 sprigs thyme
2 to 3 sprigs parsley
1 sprig rosemary
2 bay leaves

STEW:

4 small (1.4 kg/3 lb) bone-in lamb shanks, will yield about 50% meat
½ teaspoon fine sea salt, or to taste
Ground black pepper
2 tablespoons (30 g/1.1 oz) ghee or other healthy cooking fat, divided
1 medium (110 g/3.9 oz) yellow onion, chopped
2 large (128 g/4.5 oz) celery stalks, sliced
1 cup (240 ml) bone broth (page 33) or water
10.6 ounces (300 g) green beans, trimmed and halved
8.8 ounces (250 g) baby turnips, halved, or 1 regular turnip, diced
Fresh parsley for garnish

Instructions

Preheat your slow cooker. Make the bouquet garni by placing all the herbs in a piece of cheesecloth and tying with unwaxed kitchen string. This will make it easy to remove once cooked.

Season the lamb shanks with salt and pepper. To brown the lamb, grease a large heavy-based saucepan or Dutch oven with half of the ghee. Cook the lamb over high heat in batches until browned on all sides and transfer to the slow cooker.

Grease the pan with the remaining ghee. Add the onion and cook over medium-high heat for 5 to 8 minutes, until lightly browned. Add the celery and cook for a minute. Add the bone broth and bring to a boil while scraping the browned bits off the bottom. Pour into the slow cooker and cook on low for 8 hours.

After 6 hours of cooking, using tongs, transfer the lamb to a plate. Place the green beans and turnips in the slow cooker and add back the lamb. Cook for another 2 hours, or until the green beans are crisp-tender and the meat is soft and juicy. Discard the bouquet garni and garnish with fresh parsley before serving. To store, let it cool, and refrigerate for up to 4 days. To freeze, first shred the meat off the bone and freeze for up to 3 months.

NUTRITION FACTS PER SERVING:
Total carbs: 12.7 g / Fiber: 4.2 g / Net carbs: 8.5 g / Protein: 32.6 g / Fat: 44.4 g / Energy: 583 kcal
Macronutrient ratio: Calories from carbs (6%), protein (23%), fat (71%)

{ Chapter 5 }

DESSERTS

Slow cookers are great for making convenient no-fuss soups, stews, and casseroles. But what if slow cooking is not limited to savory soups and stews? By using a few simple tricks, you can make anything from crunchy granola and roasted nuts to creamy custard and even cheesecake! All of the following recipes can be made in a slow cooker.

MAKES: 4 servings
PREPARATION TIME: 10 minutes
COOKING TIME: 2 to 3 hours

Spiced Orange Pudding

If you've got a handful of basic ingredients and a few minutes to spare, it's easy to whip up this elegant, creamy citrus pudding. Topped with homemade, sugar-free cranberry sauce, it makes a great dinner-party dessert.

Ingredients

- **1½ cups (360 ml) coconut milk or heavy whipping cream**
- **5 egg yolks**
- **¼ cup (40 g/1.4 oz) powdered erythritol or Swerve**
- **1 tablespoon (6 g/0.2 oz) freshly grated orange zest or ½ teaspoon sugar-free orange extract**
- **¼ teaspoon ground cinnamon**
- **¼ teaspoon vanilla powder or 1 teaspoon sugar-free vanilla extract**
- **Pinch of salt**
- **Optional: 4 tablespoons (60 g/2.1 oz) Cranberry Sauce (page 29) on top (1 tablespoon per each custard)**

Instructions

Preheat the slow cooker. Fill it with 1 cup (240 ml) of boiling water. Place a spacer inside the slow cooker. Combine all the ingredients except the cranberry sauce, if using, in a bowl using a whisk. Pour the mixture into 4 ramekins and place them on top of the spacer. Cover the slow cooker with a lid and cook on low for 2 to 3 hours, until the custard is set. Remove the lid and let the custards cool to room temperature. Cover each ramekin with plastic wrap. Refrigerate for at least 2 hours or overnight. Once chilled, optionally top each one with a tablespoon (15 g/0.5 oz) of Cranberry Sauce (page 29).

NUTRITION FACTS PER SERVING:
Total carbs: 4.2 g / Fiber: 0.3 g / Net carbs: 3.9 g / Protein: 5.1 g / Fat: 23.7 g / Energy: 240 kcal
Macronutrient ratio: Calories from carbs (6%), protein (8%), fat (86%)

MAKES: 6 servings
PREPARATION TIME: 10 minutes
COOKING TIME: 3 to 4 hours

Carrot Cake Oatmeal

Feel like having dessert for breakfast? (Of course you do. Who doesn't?) Perk up your morning with this filling, grain-free oatmeal made with nuts, coconut, carrots, pumpkin, and warming autumn spices.

Ingredients

¼ cup (55 g/1.9 oz) virgin coconut oil
2 cups (480 ml) unsweetened almond milk or cashew milk
1 cup (240 ml) coconut milk
½ cup (100 g/3.5 oz) unsweetened pumpkin purée (page 20)
⅓ cup (83 g/2.9 oz) almond butter or coconut butter
½ cup (38 g/1.3 oz) unsweetened shredded coconut
1 cup (110 g/3.9 oz) grated carrot
½ cup (58 g/2 oz) chopped walnuts or pecans
3 tablespoons (30 g/1.1 oz) granulated erythritol or Swerve
1 teaspoon fresh lemon or orange zest
½ teaspoon vanilla powder or 2 teaspoons sugar-free vanilla extract
1 tablespoon (8 g/0.3 oz) pumpkin pie spice (or make your own, page 23)
¼ cup (38 g/1.3 oz) chia seeds
Optional: few drops of liquid stevia

OPTIONAL TOPPINGS:
Creamed coconut milk (see page 21), heavy whipping cream, or mascarpone cheese
Toasted flaked almonds or coconut
Roughly chopped pecan or walnut pieces

Instructions

Preheat the slow cooker. Place all the ingredients apart from the chia seeds in the slow cooker, and heat through for about 1 hour. When the mixture is warm, add the chia seeds and combine well. Cover with a lid and cook on low for 3 to 4 hours, stirring once or twice. When done, taste and add stevia if needed. Serve warm or cold with any optional toppings. To store, let it cool, and place in an airtight container. Store in the fridge for up to 5 days.

NUTRITION FACTS PER SERVING (¾ CUP/180 G/6.4 OZ):
Total carbs: 13.9 g / Fiber: 7.5 g / Net carbs: 6.4 g / Protein: 8.2 g / Fat: 34.3 g / Energy: 389 kcal
Macronutrient ratio: Calories from carbs (7%), protein (9%), fat (84%)

MAKES: 8 servings
PREPARATION TIME: 15 minutes
COOKING TIME: 2 to 3 hours

"Apple" Pie Crumble

There's nothing as comforting as the scent of a freshly baked apple pie on a cool fall evening, is there? With this low-carb version, which uses zucchini in place of apples, you can feel free to dig right in!

Ingredients

CRUMBLE TOPPING:

- **¼ cup (57 g/2 oz) butter or virgin coconut oil**
- **2 cups (200 g/7.1 oz) almond flour**
- **¼ cup (50 g/1.8 oz) granulated erythritol or Swerve**
- **1 teaspoon ground cinnamon**

"APPLE" PIE BASE:

- **6 (1.2 kg/2.6 lb) medium zucchini**
- **¼ cup (57 g/2 oz) butter or virgin coconut oil**
- **1 tablespoon (8 g/0.3 oz) ground cinnamon**
- **1 teaspoon vanilla powder or 1 tablespoon (15 ml) sugar-free vanilla extract**
- **1 teaspoon ground nutmeg**
- **1 tablespoon cream of tartar**
- **3 tablespoons (45 ml) fresh lemon juice**
- **½ cup (100 g/3.5 oz) granulated erythritol or Swerve**
- **Optional: few drops of liquid stevia**
- **Optional: serve with mascarpone cheese, sour cream, whipped cream, or creamed coconut milk (see page 21)**

Instructions

Preheat the slow cooker and add the butter to let it melt. To make the crumble topping, mix the almond flour, erythritol, and cinnamon. Add the butter, and use your hands to combine into a crumbly dough. Set aside.

Peel, halve, and quarter the zucchini lengthwise and cut the middle part off. Cut the zucchini into ½-inch (1-cm) thick slices and place them in the slow cooker. Add the butter, cinnamon, vanilla, nutmeg, cream of tartar, lemon juice, erythritol, and optional stevia. Using a spatula, combine the zucchini with all the spices, and then add the crumble topping.

Place 2 layers of high-absorbent paper towels or a tea towel on top of the ceramic bowl and cover with a lid. Cook on low for 2 to 3 hours, until the zucchini is tender. Serve with mascarpone cheese, sour cream, whipped cream, or creamed coconut milk. To store, place in an airtight container, and refrigerate for up to 5 days or freeze in manageable servings for up to 6 months.

NUTRITION FACTS PER SERVING:
Total carbs: 9 g / Fiber: 3.6 g / Net carbs: 5.4 g / Protein: 5.7 g / Fat: 20.1 g / Energy: 226 kcal
Macronutrient ratio: Calories from carbs (10%), protein (10%), fat (80%)

MAKES: 4 servings
PREPARATION TIME: 10 minutes
COOKING TIME: 2 to 3 hours + chilling

Snickerdoodle Crème Brûlée

If there's a single dessert in this world that's made for a slow cooker, it's got to be crème brûlée. This foolproof method results in evenly cooked, creamy custards with perfectly crispy tops.

Ingredients

- **2 cups (480 ml) coconut milk or heavy whipping cream**
- **5 egg yolks**
- **¼ cup (40 g/1.4 oz) powdered erythritol or Swerve, plus 4 teaspoons granulated erythritol or Swerve for topping**
- **1 teaspoon ground cinnamon**
- **½ teaspoon vanilla powder or 2 teaspoons sugar-free vanilla extract**
- **Pinch of salt**

Instructions

Preheat the slow cooker and fill it with 1 cup (240 ml) of boiling water. Place a spacer inside the slow cooker. Combine all the ingredients, apart from the 4 teaspoons of erythritol, in a bowl using a whisk. Pour the mixture into 4 ramekins and place them on top of the spacer, cover the slow cooker with a lid, and cook on low for 2 to 3 hours, until the custard is set. Remove the lid and let the custards cool to room temperature. Cover each ramekin with plastic wrap. Refrigerate for at least 2 hours or overnight.

When ready to serve, sprinkle each one with a teaspoon of granulated erythritol or Swerve (see tip below). Place under a broiler set to high for 3 to 5 minutes to caramelize, or use a blowtorch.

TIP: You can use Swerve to make the caramelized topping. Although erythritol will create a hard shell, it will not brown. Swerve contains fructooligosaccharides, which will help the tops brown and create the sugar effect.

NUTRITION FACTS PER SERVING:
Total carbs: 5 g / Fiber: 0.3 g / Net carbs: 4.7 g / Protein: 5.7 g / Fat: 29.8 g / Energy: 295 kcal
Macronutrient ratio: Calories from carbs (6%), protein (7%), fat (87%)

MAKES: 4 servings
PREPARATION TIME: 10 minutes
COOKING TIME: 2 to 3 hours + chilling

Pumpkin Pie Custard

The best part of pumpkin pie is the smooth, spiced, spoonable filling, so I came up with this no-fuss keto version of everyone's favorite fall treat. Like the Snickerdoodle Crème Brûlée on page 81, making it in your slow cooker results in the ideal texture—no guesswork required.

Ingredients

CUSTARDS:

1 cup (240 ml) coconut milk or heavy whipping cream
1 cup (200 g/7.1 oz) unsweetened pumpkin purée (make your own, page 20)
2 large eggs
¼ cup (40 g/1.4 oz) powdered erythritol or Swerve
1 teaspoon pumpkin pie spice (make your own, page 23)
½ teaspoon vanilla powder or 2 teaspoons unsweetened vanilla extract
Pinch of salt

TOPPING:

½ cup (120 g/4.2 oz) creamed coconut milk or mascarpone cheese
2 tablespoons (30 ml) liquid coconut milk or heavy whipping cream
¼ teaspoon ground cinnamon
Optional: few drops of liquid stevia

Instructions

Preheat the slow cooker. Fill it with 1 cup (240 ml) of boiling water. Place a spacer inside the slow cooker. Combine all the custard ingredients in a bowl using a whisk. Pour the mixture into 4 ramekins and place the ramekins on top of the spacer. Cover the slow cooker with a lid and cook on low for 2 to 3 hours, until the custard is set. Remove the lid and let the custards cool to room temperature. Cover each ramekin with plastic wrap. Refrigerate for at least 2 hours or overnight.

To make the topping, combine the creamed coconut milk, liquid coconut milk, cinnamon, and optionally a few drops of stevia. When the custards are chilled, top each one with a dollop of the prepared topping.

NUTRITION FACTS PER SERVING:
Total carbs: 8.9 g / Fiber: 2.4 g / Net carbs: 6.5 g / Protein: 6 g / Fat: 25 g / Energy: 268 kcal
Macronutrient ratio: Calories from carbs (9%), protein (9%), fat (82%)

MAKES: 20 servings
PREPARATION TIME: 15 minutes
COOKING TIME: 2 to 3 hours

Chocolate Chip Cookie Bites

Need to make a big batch of cookies in a matter of minutes? No problem! This recipe for keto cookies couldn't be easier, and the result is a perfectly bite-size treat that's delicious with a dollop of whipped cream, coconut cream, or yogurt.

Ingredients

2 cups (500 g/1.1 lb) almond butter or nut butter of choice
1 cup (250 g/8.8 oz) coconut butter, or more nut butter
2 large eggs
2 egg yolks
½ cup (100 g/3.5 oz) granulated erythritol or Swerve
½ teaspoon fine sea salt
1 tablespoon freshly grated lemon or orange zest
1 teaspoon vanilla powder or ground cinnamon
2 teaspoons gluten-free baking powder
1 cup (100 g/3.5 oz) pecan or walnut halves, chopped
3.5 ounces (100 g) dark chocolate chips or chopped chocolate bar (minimum 85% cacao)
Suggested topping: whipped cream or creamed coconut milk

Instructions

Line the slow cooker with heavy-duty parchment paper. Preheat the cooker to low.

Place the almond butter, coconut butter, eggs, egg yolks, erythritol, salt, lemon zest, vanilla, and baking powder in a food processor. Pulse for a few seconds until well combined. Transfer the dough to the slow cooker and add the pecan halves and chocolate chips, pressing them into the dough and spreading the dough evenly. Cover and cook for 2 to 3 hours on low, flipping the bowl halfway through to ensure even cooking.

When done, turn the slow cooker off and remove the lid. Let it sit in the slow cooker for at least 2 hours. Cut into 20 pieces, and let the cookie bites cool completely. Instead of slicing, you can simply spoon a serving (about 65 g/2.3 oz) of cookie crumbles into a bowl and serve with whipped cream or creamed coconut milk. Transfer to a container. Store uncovered at room temperature for up to 1 week, or freeze for up to 6 months.

NUTRITION FACTS PER SERVING:
Total carbs: 9.9 g / Fiber: 5.7 g / Net carbs: 4.2 g / Protein: 7.7 g / Fat: 25.9 g / Energy: 311 kcal
Macronutrient ratio: Calories from carbs (6%), protein (11%), fat (83%)

MAKES: 13 servings
PREPARATION TIME: 10 minutes
COOKING TIME: 2 to 3 hours + chilling

Macadamia Chai Cake

If your go-to coffee shop treat is a chai tea latte, you'll adore this gently spiced quick-prep slow cooker cake. It's incredibly nutritious, too, because it's packed with macadamias, which are high in B vitamins and minerals like iron, magnesium, and manganese.

Ingredients

CHAI SPICE MIX:

½ teaspoon vanilla powder
½ teaspoon ground cinnamon
½ teaspoon ground nutmeg
½ teaspoon ground cloves
½ teaspoon ground cardamom
½ teaspoon ground allspice
¼ teaspoon ginger powder
¼ teaspoon fennel seeds

CAKE:

¾ cup (188 g/6.6 oz) coconut butter (a.k.a. coconut manna)
1 cup (134 g/4.7 oz) macadamia nuts
½ cup (100 g/3.5 oz) granulated erythritol, Swerve, or brown sugar substitute such as Sukrin
1 cup (240 ml) coconut milk, at room temperature
4 large eggs
2 teaspoons gluten-free baking powder
Pinch of fine sea salt
Optional: few drops of liquid stevia

Instructions

Line the slow cooker with heavy-duty parchment paper. Preheat the cooker to low. Prepare the spice mix by mixing all the ingredients.

Place the coconut butter and macadamias in a food processor, and process until smooth. Add the erythritol, coconut milk, eggs, baking powder, salt, and optionally a few drops of stevia. Process for a few seconds until well combined.

Transfer the dough to the slow cooker. Cover, and cook on low for 2 to 3 hours. When done, remove the lid and let the cake cool. Grab the parchment paper to remove it from the slow cooker and slice. Keep at room temperature for up to 3 days, or freeze for up to 6 months.

NUTRITION FACTS PER SERVING:
Total carbs: 6.3 g / Fiber: 3.4 g / Net carbs: 2.9 g / Protein: 4 g / Fat: 21 g / Energy: 217 kcal
Macronutrient ratio: Calories from carbs (5%), protein (7%), fat (88%)

MAKES: 13 servings
PREPARATION TIME: 15 minutes
COOKING TIME: 2 to 3 hours + chilling

Lemon Drizzle Cake

Looking for a summery, tangy, guilt-free dessert? This no-starch citrus cake is the answer: it's my low-carb take on English celebrity chef Mary Berry's legendary lemon drizzle cake.

Ingredients

CAKE:

- **2 cups (200 g/7.1 oz) almond flour**
- **⅓ cup (40 g/1.4 oz) coconut flour**
- **½ cup (100 g/3.5 oz) granulated erythritol or Swerve**
- **¼ cup (25 g/0.9 oz) unflavored or vanilla whey protein powder or egg white protein powder**
- **2 teaspoons gluten-free baking powder**
- **½ teaspoon vanilla bean powder or 2 teaspoons sugar-free vanilla extract**
- **½ cup (120 ml) almond milk, at room temperature**
- **½ cup (114 g/4 oz) butter or coconut oil, melted**
- **6 large eggs, at room temperature**
- **Zest of 2 lemons (about 2 tablespoons or 12 g)**
- **Optional: few drops of stevia**

LEMON DRIZZLE TOPPING:

- **¼ cup (50 g/1.8 oz) granulated erythritol or Swerve**
- **¼ cup (60 ml) hot water**
- **Juice from 2 lemons (about 60 ml/½ cup)**
- **1 tablespoon (10 g/0.4 oz) powdered erythritol or Swerve, for dusting**

Instructions

Line the slow cooker with heavy-duty parchment paper. Preheat the cooker to low. In a bowl, mix all the dry ingredients for the cake: almond flour, coconut flour, erythritol, protein powder, baking powder, and vanilla powder. In a mixer, process the almond milk, melted butter, eggs, lemon zest, and optionally a few drops of stevia. Slowly sift the prepared dry mixture into the wet mixture until well combined.

Pour the dough in the slow cooker. Cover, and cook on low for 2 to 3 hours. When done, remove the lid and let the cake cool for a few minutes.

Prepare the lemon drizzle. Dissolve the erythritol in a small saucepan with the hot water, and then add the lemon juice. Use the back of a spoon and drizzle it over the cake. Let it sit for 1 to 2 hours. Grab the parchment paper to remove the cake from the slow cooker. Use a fine-mesh sieve to sprinkle the powdered erythritol over the cake and slice it. Keep at room temperature for up to 3 days, or freeze for up to 6 months.

NUTRITION FACTS PER SERVING:
Total carbs: 5.6 g / Fiber: 2.2 g / Net carbs: 3.4 g / Protein: 8.7 g / Fat: 18 g / Energy: 212 kcal
Macronutrient ratio: Calories from carbs (6%), protein (17%), fat (77%)

MAKES: 13 servings
PREPARATION TIME: 20 minutes
COOKING TIME: 2 to 3 hours + cooling

Spiced Chocolate & Coconut Cake

This cake is based on a Czech cake called pernik. Its unique mixture of warming spices makes it very special, and while it's usually baked in the oven, I think its texture actually improves when it's prepared in a slow cooker.

Ingredients

PERNIK SPICE MIX:

2 tablespoons (16 g/0.6 oz) ground cinnamon
1 tablespoon (5 g/0.2 oz) ground ginger
1½ teaspoons ground cloves
1½ teaspoons ground allspice
1 teaspoon ground coriander
½ teaspoon star anise powder
½ teaspoon vanilla powder
¼ teaspoon ground cardamom
¼ teaspoon ground nutmeg
¼ teaspoon fennel seeds
⅛ teaspoon cayenne pepper

CAKE:

1 cup (120 g/4.2 oz) coconut flour
1¼ cups (100 g/3.5 oz) ground walnuts, pecans, or sunflower seeds
¾ cup (150 g/5.3 oz) granulated erythritol or Swerve
½ cup (43 g/1.5 oz) cacao powder
1 tablespoon (7 g/0.3 oz) gelatin powder
1 tablespoon (12 g/0.4 oz) gluten-free baking powder

Instructions

Line the slow cooker with heavy-duty parchment paper. Preheat the cooker to low. Prepare the spice mix by combining all the ingredients. (Store the leftover spice mix in an airtight container.)

In a bowl, mix all the dry ingredients for the cake: coconut flour, ground walnuts, erythritol, cacao powder, gelatin, baking powder, and 1 tablespoon plus 1 teaspoon (13 g/0.5 oz) of the prepared spice mix. In a mixer, process the coconut milk, melted butter, eggs, lemon zest, and optionally a few drops of stevia. Slowly sift in the prepared dry mixture until well combined.

Transfer the dough to the slow cooker and spread it evenly with a spatula. Cover and cook on low for 2 to 3 hours, until set. When done, remove the lid and let the cake cool for several hours.

Prepare the topping. Break the chocolate into pieces and place in a bowl with the spice mix. Heat the cream and butter over medium heat. When hot, pour over the chocolate. Mix until smooth and creamy. Pour on top of the cake, sprinkle with the shredded coconut, and let it sit for 1 to 2 hours. Grab the parchment paper to remove the cake from the slow cooker and slice. Place in an airtight container. Refrigerate for up to 5 days, or freeze for up to 6 months. Any leftover pernik spice mix should be stored in an airtight container for up to a year.

Nutrition facts per serving:
Total carbs: 11.5 g / Fiber: 5.3 g / Net carbs: 6.2 g / Protein: 9.4 g / Fat: 28.2 g / Energy: 325 kcal
Macronutrient ratio: Calories from carbs (8%), protein (12%), fat (80%)

1 tablespoon plus 1 teaspoon (13 g/0.5 oz) pernik spice mix
1 cup (240 ml) coconut milk, at room temperature
½ cup (114 g/4 oz) butter or coconut oil, melted
6 large eggs, at room temperature
1 tablespoon (6 g/0.2 oz) freshly grated lemon or orange zest, or 1 teaspoon sugar-free lemon or orange extract
Optional: few drops of liquid stevia

TOPPING:

3.5 ounces (100 g) dark chocolate (minimum 85% cacao)
½ teaspoon pernik spice mix
¼ cup plus 2 tablespoons (90 ml) coconut milk or heavy whipping cream
3 tablespoons (43 g/1.5 oz) butter or coconut oil
1 cup (75 g/2.7 oz) unsweetened shredded coconut

MAKES: 13 servings
PREPARATION TIME: 20 minutes
COOKING TIME: 2 to 3 hours + chilling

Chocolate Hazelnut Cake

Nutella, the famous chocolate-hazelnut spread adored by kids and grown-ups alike, is packed with sugar, so you'll need to avoid it if you follow a keto or low-carb lifestyle. But the good news is that you can enjoy its sweet-and-nutty taste in this simple, sugar-free chocolate cake.

Ingredients

CAKE:

- **2 cups (200 g/7.1 oz) almond flour**
- **1⅓ cups (100 g/3.5 oz) ground peeled hazelnuts (see tip below)**
- **¾ cup (150 g/5.3 oz) granulated erythritol or Swerve**
- **½ cup (43 g/1.5 oz) cacao powder**
- **1 teaspoon vanilla bean powder or 1 tablespoon sugar-free vanilla extract**
- **2 teaspoons gluten-free baking powder**
- **1 cup (240 ml) almond or hazelnut milk, at room temperature**
- **½ cup (114 g/4 oz) butter or coconut oil, melted**
- **4 large eggs, at room temperature**
- **Optional: few drops of liquid stevia**

Instructions

Line the slow cooker with heavy-duty parchment paper. Preheat the cooker to low. In a bowl, mix all the dry ingredients for the cake: almond flour, ground hazelnuts (see tip on how to peel them before grinding), erythritol, cacao powder, vanilla, and baking powder. In a mixer, process the almond milk, melted butter, eggs, and optionally a few drops of stevia. Slowly sift the prepared dry mixture into the wet mixture until well combined.

Pour the batter into the slow cooker. Cover, and cook on low for 2 to 3 hours. When done, remove the lid and let the cake cool.

Prepare the topping. Break the chocolate into small pieces and place in a bowl with the vanilla. Heat the cream and butter over medium heat. When hot, pour over the chocolate. Mix until smooth and creamy. Pour on top of the cake, sprinkle with the roasted hazelnuts, and let it sit for 1 to 2 hours. Grab the parchment paper to remove the cake from the slow cooker and slice. To store, place in an airtight container. Refrigerate for up to 5 days or freeze for up to 6 months.

TIP: To roast and peel hazelnuts: Preheat the oven to 375°F (190°C, or gas mark 5). Spread the hazelnuts on a baking sheet. Place in the oven and bake for about 10 minutes. Remove from the oven and cool for 15 minutes. Rub the hazelnuts in your hands to remove the skins (these would taste bitter). Grind them into a fine powder in a food processor.

Nutrition facts per serving:
Total carbs: 10.8 g / Fiber: 4.9 g / Net carbs: 5.9 g / Protein: 9.5 g / Fat: 35 g / Energy: 371 kcal
Macronutrient ratio: Calories from carbs (6%), protein (10%), fat (84%)

TOPPING:

3.5 ounces (100 g) dark chocolate (minimum 85% cacao)

½ teaspoon vanilla bean powder or 2 teaspoons sugar-free vanilla extract

¼ cup plus 2 tablespoons (90 ml) coconut milk or heavy whipping cream

3 tablespoons (43 g/1.5 oz) butter or coconut oil

1 cup (115 g/4.1 oz) chopped roasted hazelnuts

MAKES: 13 servings
PREPARATION TIME: 20 minutes
COOKING TIME: 3 to 4 hours

Brownie Almond Cheesecake Bars

This luscious keto treat is the perfect marriage of two popular desserts—almond cheesecake and dark, fudgy chocolate brownies—and you won't believe they're actually sugar-free. Serve with a hot cup of coffee or tea.

Ingredients

CHEESECAKE LAYER:

- **1 cup (240 g/8.5 oz) full-fat cream cheese, at room temperature**
- **¼ cup (58 g/2 oz) full-fat sour cream**
- **½ cup (125 g/4.4 oz) almond butter, softened**
- **1 egg yolk**
- **1 large egg**
- **¼ cup (40 g/1.4 oz) powdered erythritol or Swerve**
- **½ teaspoon ground cinnamon**
- **1 teaspoon sugar-free almond extract**
- **Optional: few drops of liquid stevia**

BROWNIE LAYER:

- **3.5 ounces (100 g) dark chocolate (minimum 85% cacao)**
- **4.4 ounces (125 g) butter or coconut oil, melted**
- **3 large eggs**
- **¾ cup (120 g/4.2 oz) powdered erythritol or Swerve**
- **1 cup (100 g/3.5 oz) almond flour**
- **½ cup (43 g/1.5 oz) cacao powder**
- **¼ cup (32 g/1.1 oz) ground chia seeds**
- **2 teaspoons gluten-free baking powder**
- **¼ teaspoon fine sea salt**

Instructions

Line the slow cooker with heavy-duty parchment paper. Preheat the cooker to low. Place all the cheesecake ingredients in a mixing bowl: cream cheese, sour cream, softened almond butter, egg yolk, egg, erythritol, cinnamon, almond extract, and optionally a few drops of stevia. Set aside.

To prepare the brownie layer, break the chocolate into pieces and add to a heatproof bowl with the butter. Place over a pan filled with simmering water and make sure the water doesn't touch the bowl: only the steam should heat the bowl. Slowly melt while stirring. When most of the chocolate is melted, remove the pan from the burner and let the mixture continue to melt. Set aside.

Place the eggs and powdered erythritol in another bowl and whisk until well combined. Beat in the chocolate mixture and gently fold in the almond flour, cacao powder, ground chia seeds, baking powder, and salt, and process well.

Pour the brownie batter into the slow cooker and spread evenly. Top with the prepared cheesecake mixture. Cover and cook on low for 3 to 4 hours. When done, remove the lid and let cool. Once cooled, grab the parchment paper to remove the cake from the slow cooker, and slice. To store, place in an airtight container. Refrigerate for up to 5 days or freeze for up to 6 months.

NUTRITION FACTS PER SERVING:
Total carbs: 10 g / Fiber: 4.6 g / Net carbs: 5.4 g / Protein: 9 g / Fat: 29.3 g / Energy: 323 kcal
Macronutrient ratio: Calories from carbs (7%), protein (11%), fat (82%)

MAKES: 12 servings
PREPARATION TIME: 30 minutes
COOKING TIME: 4 hours + chilling

New York Cheesecake with Chocolate Ganache

This classic deli-style dessert is rich, creamy, satisfying—and, of course, completely starch-free. And it's so simple: "baking" the cake in your slow cooker yields a perfectly creamy texture each and every time.

Ingredients

CRUST:

- **1 cup (100 g/3.5 oz) almond flour**
- **2 tablespoons (28 g/1 oz) butter or virgin coconut oil**
- **¼ cup (40 g/1.4 oz) powdered erythritol or Swerve**
- **1 egg yolk**
- **½ teaspoon vanilla bean powder or ground cinnamon**
- **Pinch of fine sea salt**

CHEESECAKE LAYER:

- **2 cups (480 g/16.9 oz) full-fat cream cheese, at room temperature**
- **½ cup (114 g/4 oz) full-fat sour cream**
- **1 egg yolk**
- **1 large egg**
- **½ cup (80 g/2.8 oz) powdered erythritol or Swerve**
- **½ teaspoon vanilla bean powder or 2 teaspoons sugar-free vanilla extract**
- **2 tablespoons (30 ml) fresh lemon juice**
- **1 teaspoon fresh lemon zest**

Instructions

Preheat a 5- to 6-quart (4.7- to 5.7-L) slow cooker and fill with 1 cup (240 ml) of boiling water. Place a spacer inside the slow cooker. Line the bottom of a medium springform pan with parchment paper. Make sure the springform pan fits in the slow cooker and the bottom doesn't touch the water.

Combine all the ingredients for the crust: almond flour, butter, erythritol, egg yolk, vanilla, and salt. Mix using your hands and press into the bottom of the springform pan. Set aside while you prepare the cheesecake layer.

In a bowl, using a whisk or an electric mixer, mix the cream cheese, sour cream, egg yolk, egg, erythritol, vanilla, lemon juice, lemon zest, and coconut flour. Optionally, add a few drops of stevia. Pour into the springform pan over the almond crust.

Place the springform pan in the slow cooker on top of the spacer. Cover, and cook on low for 4 hours. When done, turn off the heat, remove the lid, and let cool. Leave the cheesecake in the slow cooker to cool for 2 to 3 hours. Refrigerate in the springform pan overnight. When ready to make the chocolate ganache, gently remove the cheesecake from the springform pan by running the side of a blunt knife between the edge of the cheesecake and the pan.

Prepare the chocolate ganache. Break the chocolate into small pieces and place in a bowl with the vanilla. Heat the cream and butter over medium heat and, when hot, pour over the chocolate.

NUTRITION FACTS PER SERVING:
Total carbs: 6.9 g / Fiber: 1.8 g / Net carbs: 5.1 g / Protein: 7.6 g / Fat: 29.3 g / Energy: 295 kcal
Macronutrient ratio: Calories from carbs (6%), protein (10%), fat (84%)

1 heaped tablespoon (12 g/0.4 oz) coconut flour
Optional: few drops of liquid stevia

GANACHE:

3.5 ounces (100 g) dark chocolate (minimum 85% cacao)
½ teaspoon vanilla bean powder or 2 teaspoons sugar-free vanilla extract
¼ cup plus 2 tablespoons (90 ml) heavy whipping cream or coconut milk
3 tablespoons (43 g/1.5 oz) butter or coconut oil
Optional: few drops of liquid stevia

Mix until smooth and creamy. Leave to cool slightly, and then pour over the cheesecake. Let it chill in the fridge for at least 10 minutes before slicing. Store in an airtight container in the fridge for up to 5 days or freeze for up to 6 months.

TIP: Don't panic if the ganache separates. You can fix it by placing it in a blender or a food processor with 1 to 2 tablespoons (15 to 30 ml) of hot water. Process until smooth and creamy.

MAKES: 16 servings (about 8 cups)
PREPARATION TIME: 10 minutes
COOKING TIME: 3 to 4 hours

Spiced Bacon Granola

Bacon goes with absolutely everything, and that includes this nutty, crunchy, grain-free breakfast granola. The bacon lends it a savory twist, but it's also lightly sweet and super-satisfying.

Ingredients

- 6 slices (180 g/6.4 oz) unsmoked bacon
- ½ cup (120 ml) water
- 2 tablespoons (30 g/1.1 oz) extra-virgin coconut oil
- ¼ cup (63 g/2.2 oz) almond butter or coconut butter
- 1½ cups (90 g/3.2 oz) unsweetened coconut flakes
- ¾ cup (56 g/2 oz) unsweetened shredded coconut
- 1 cup (140 g/5 oz) whole almonds, roughly chopped
- 1 cup (100 g/3.5 oz) pecan or walnut halves, roughly chopped
- ½ cup (65 g/2.3 oz) pumpkin seeds or sunflower seeds
- 2 tablespoons (16 g/0.6 oz) chia seeds or flax seeds
- 1 tablespoon (8 g/0.3 oz) ground cinnamon
- 1 teaspoon vanilla powder or 1 tablespoon (15 ml) sugar-free vanilla extract
- ¼ cup (50 g/1.8 oz) granulated erythritol or Swerve (can be skipped)
- Suggestions: serve with unsweetened nut milk (page 21), coconut milk, or yogurt

Instructions

Preheat the slow cooker. Place the bacon pieces in a large pan and add the water. Cook over medium-high heat until the water starts to boil. Reduce the heat to medium and cook until the water evaporates and the bacon fat is rendered. Reduce the heat to low and cook until the bacon is lightly browned and crispy. Set aside.

Place the coconut oil and almond butter in the slow cooker and let it melt. In a bowl, mix the coconut flakes, shredded coconut, almond and pecan pieces, pumpkin seeds, chia seeds, cinnamon, vanilla, and erythritol. Place all the ingredients, including the crisped-up bacon and bacon grease, in the slow cooker, and combine using a spatula. Cover with a lid and cook on low for 3 to 4 hours, mixing every hour to prevent burning. When done, let the granola cool, and then transfer to a jar. Store at room temperature for up to 1 month. Serve with coconut milk, almond milk, or full-fat yogurt.

NUTRITION FACTS PER SERVING (½ CUP/40 G/1.4 OZ):
Total carbs: 7.1 g / Fiber: 4.5 g / Net carbs: 2.6 g / Protein: 7.2 g / Fat: 21.6 g / Energy: 244 kcal
Macronutrient ratio: Calories from carbs (4%), protein (13%), fat (83%)